OLDSMOBILE
W-POWERED
MUSCLE CARS

David Newhardt

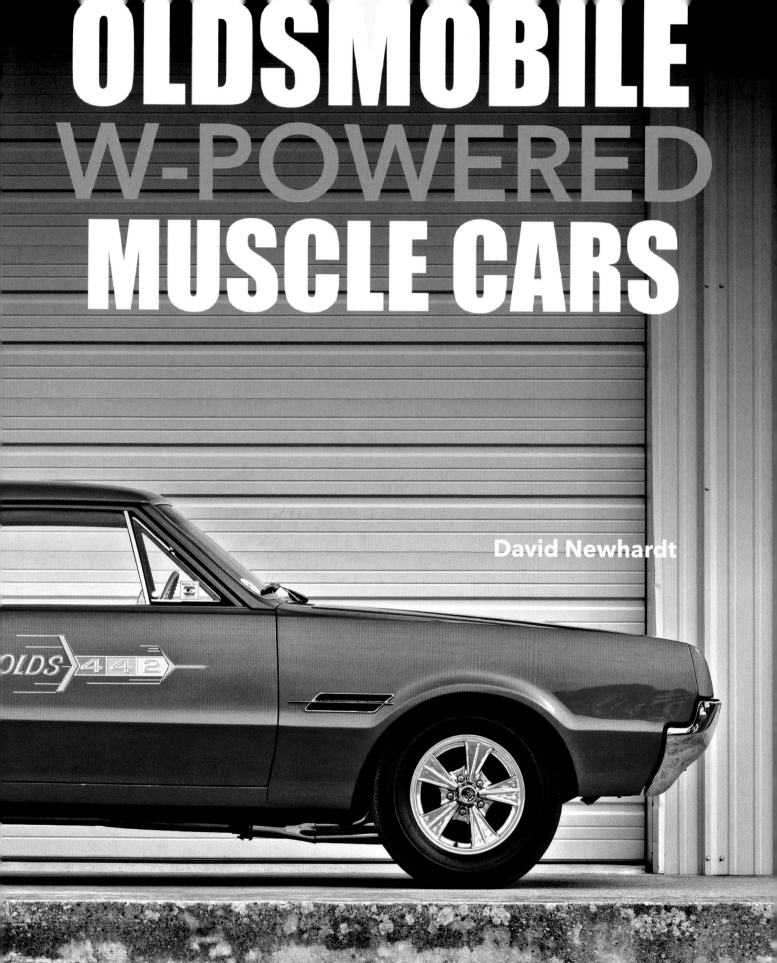

CarTech®

CarTech®, Inc.
838 Lake Street South
Forest Lake, MN 55025
Phone: 651-277-1200 or 800-551-4754
Fax: 651-277-1203
www.cartechbooks.com

Edit by Wes Eisenschenk
Layout by Connie DeFlorin

ISBN 978-1-61325-540-7
Item No. CT667

Library of Congress Cataloging-in-Publication Data

Names: Newhardt, David, 1955- author.
Title: Oldsmobile W-powered muscle cars : includes W-30, W-31, W-32, W-33, W-34, and more / David Newhardt.
Description: Forest Lake, MN : CarTech, Inc., [2021] | "Item No. CT667."
Identifiers: LCCN 2021058720 | ISBN 9781613255407 (hardback)
Subjects: LCSH: Oldsmobile automobile–History–20th century. | Muscle cars–United States–History–20th century.
Classification: LCC TL215.O4 .N49 2021 | DDC 629.222–dc23
LC record available at https://lccn.loc.gov/2021058720

Written, edited, and designed in the U.S.A.
Printed in China
10 9 8 7 6 5 4 3 2 1

DISTRIBUTION BY:

Europe
PGUK
63 Hatton Garden
London EC1N 8LE, England
Phone: 020 7061 1980 • Fax: 020 7242 3725
www.pguk.co.uk

Australia
Renniks Publications Ltd.
3/37-39 Green Street
Banksmeadow, NSW 2109, Australia
Phone: 2 9695 7055 • Fax: 2 9695 7355
www.renniks.com

Canada
Login Canada
300 Saulteaux Crescent
Winnipeg, MB, R3J 3T2 Canada
Phone: 800 665 1148 • Fax: 800 665 0103
www.lb.ca

TABLE OF CONTENTS

Foreword
Jerry Wilson - President of the Oldsmobile Club of America

Oldsmobile has a long history of innovation and building performance cars. The W-Machines were descendants of a series of automobiles that had established a legacy of speed that reached back more than 60 years when the first 442 was introduced.

Ransom Eli Olds created his first horseless carriage in 1887. It was powered by steam. That vehicle was succeeded by a gasoline-powered horseless carriage in 1897, and there was even an electric-powered Olds that was shown at the 1901 Chicago Auto Show.

One of the key figures in early automobile racing was Alexander Winton. He sold his first automobile in 1898 and recognized that racing was an effective and profitable approach to advertising the new machines. In 1902, he built the first of three *Bullet* race cars. In September 1902 at a horse racing track in Cleveland, Ohio, the he drove the *Bullet* 10 miles in less than 11 minutes. In October 1902 in Grosse Pointe, Michigan, he drove the *Bullet* in a contest with Henry Ford's *999* (driven by Barney Oldfield) and lost when the *Bullet* began to misfire. In March 1903 at Ormond Beach, Florida, he drove the *Bullet* in a race with the Olds *Pirate* (driven by H. T. Thomas) at the Ormond Challenge Cup at the first Florida Winter Speed Carnival. The *Pirate* lost by two-tenths of a second but established a legacy for Oldsmobile.

In 1949, Oldsmobile created what would be considered by many to be the first muscle car. The Futuramic 88 was a combination of the body from a relatively light 76 Series with a 6-cylinder engine along with the V-8 engine from the 98 Series. For the next few years, Oldsmobile and Hudson dominated the National Association for Stock Car Auto Racing (NASCAR).

Through the 1950s, Chrysler, Ford, and General Motors all made significant advances in the development of horsepower, and the NASCAR rules evolved in an effort to maintain parity for competitors. Chrysler was developing larger-displacement, higher-compression engines with hemispherical heads and spurred Oldsmobile into action. Oldsmobile recognized that increasing the displacement from 324 to 371 ci and increasing the compression to 10.0:1 were not sufficient to maintain its competitive edge. As a result, Oldsmobile developed an optional multiple-carburetor setup (J2 Triple Carburetion package), which made it available for NASCAR racing.

Oldsmobile retained Lee Petty to drive the J2 Oldsmobile for the 1957 NASCAR season. However, in mid-season, multiple carburetors were banned, so Oldsmobile completed the season using a single carburetor. The J2 package was available for production cars in the 1957 and 1958 model years and then was discontinued.

In 1957, the Automobile Manufacturers Association recommended that automobile manufacturers reduce their focus on high power and racing and increase their efforts for safety. In response, automobile manufacturers changed some of their programs and refocused their efforts of engineering. However, the demand for high horsepower did not go away and neither did the engineers who had been involved with the development and refinement of high-performance automobiles.

In the early 1960s, the Big Three manufacturers introduced compact cars that were significantly smaller than the automobiles that had evolved through the late 1950s. Again, the automotive engineers saw an opportunity to mount large engines in smaller cars as Oldsmobile had done in 1949 in response to a pent-up demand for sporty automobiles. As a result, Chrysler Corporation, Ford Motor Company, and General Motors designed and produced automobiles that responded to the growing interest in performance cars. The leaders in those efforts were Pontiac (with the 1964 GTO that had a large engine based on the Tempest) and Ford (with the 1964½ Mustang that had a new body based on a Falcon platform).

Recognizing the success of the GTO, Oldsmobile responded with an option package for the F-85 with the Police Apprehender Pursuit Package (Option B09), which included a 4-barrel carburetor, 4-speed transmission, and dual exhaust. The name of this option: 4-4-2.

This option was made available during the 1964 model year, and 2,999 were built (including 10 four-door models). Production increased to 25,003 in the 1965 model year.

In 1966, Oldsmobile introduced the W-30 option and was available for drag racing. Only 54 of these cars were built by Oldsmobile. However, Oldsmobile also offered a Track Pack option that included all of the same parts that could be added to a 4-4-2. These cars looked the same and performed the same as the W-30s built by Oldsmobile. Details of this option are provided in this book.

This book captures and illustrates the history of the development of a special series of high-performance Oldsmobiles that carry the W designation.

Oldsmobile Becomes a Muscle Car Manufacturer

For every cause, there's an effect. Oldsmobile's reaction to the GTO was the 4-4-2. With the 4-4-2, Oldsmobile had its muscle car, equipped with a 4-barrel carburetor (4), a floor-shifted manual 4-speed transmission (4), and dual exhaust (2). (Photo Courtesy General Motors)

Pontiac created the Oldsmobile 442. By building the Pontiac GTO for the 1964 model year, Oldsmobile leadership in Lansing, Michigan, felt that it had nothing to compete against in the emerging youth market. Understand that the divisions within General Motors fought each other as furiously as they battled Ford and Chrysler. With the release of the GTO, Pontiac enjoyed a considerable sales bump with a car that was created using essentially off-the-shelf components. Yet, the response in the marketplace was impressive with 32,450 units sold.

The GTO was merely an option package for the 1964 Pontiac Tempest, and it bucked the rules within General Motors regarding the size of an engine in a midsize platform. John DeLorean was the young, brash wunderkind of Pontiac, and he and Pontiac General Manager Elliot "Pete" Estes pushed the GTO through to production. The sales manager of Pontiac, Frank Bridges, was convinced that no more than 5,000 would sell. When the public embraced the GTO and money started flowing into GM's coffers, Bridges conceded that DeLorean was right. Pride was set aside in the drive for sales, and Pontiac tasked the Tempest's optional GTO package with drawing in younger buyers than would normally be seen in Pontiac's showrooms.

Unlike Pontiac, which had been active in high-profile drag racing since the late 1950s, Oldsmobile wasn't exactly known for straight-line performance. Years before muscle cars were a gleam in anyone's eye, Oldsmobile was collecting checkered flags. NASCAR debuted its Strictly Stock class in 1949, and Robert "Red" Byron took the championship that year in an Oldsmobile. That year, Oldsmobile vehicles dominated the class, winning five of the eight Grand National races.

In 1950, the Oldsmobile 88 was the big dog on NASCAR tracks, winning 10 out of 19 races. That same year, an Oldsmobile 88 driven by Hershel McGriff won the grueling 2,000-mile Carrera Panamericana road race. Heck, four of the first seven cars to finish were Oldsmobiles! In 1958, Lee Petty won the NASCAR championship in an Oldsmobile, as well as the inaugural Daytona 500 in 1959. No one could say that Oldsmobile didn't know how to build a fast car.

Time for a Response

It didn't take long for Oldsmobile's general manager and GM Vice President Jack F. Wolfram to rally the troops and quickly prepare a response to the Pontiac A-Body. Wolfram had been the chief engineer at Oldsmobile from 1944 to 1950, taking the reins as general manager in 1951; Harold Metzel became chief engineer at that time.

When it became clear that Pontiac's experiment with the GTO was a success, all hands were on deck for Oldsmobile to respond. In February 1963, Oldsmobile showed its F-85 concept car, the J-TR at the Chicago Auto Show. The J-TR had several styling cues that later made it to production. Design of the J-TR was overseen by GM Styling Chief Bill Mitchell, and the car was a head-turner, complete with Cibié rectangular headlights, split front and rear bumpers, and a racing stripe. But Oldsmobile needed a GTO fighter—and now!

Power Play

Wolfram tasked brilliant engineer John Beltz to work with Oldsmobile Chief Engineer Bob Dorshimer and Special Projects Manager Dale Smith to quickly create a solid competitor to the GTO. Starting in 1947, Beltz had worked his way up through the Oldsmobile ranks, and by the late 1950s, he was an assistant chief engineer at the division. He pushed for a front-wheel-drive sedan, and the project evolved into the Toronado. A car-guy to the core, Beltz looked at the opportunity to build a GTO fighter with relish. As events showed, he was Oldsmobile's version of John DeLorean but without the ego and vices. He worked within the system to create wonderfully memorable vehicles.

Much like the Pontiac effort, the Oldsmobile team used existing components to pare down costs and hasten development. Speed was of the essence; Oldsmobile didn't have any idea what Chevrolet and Buick were working on. The Oldsmobile team started with the same front-engine, rear-wheel-drive (FR) layout A-Body intermediate platform that Pontiac, Chevrolet, and Buick used.

The Oldsmobile F-85/Cutlass was all-new for 1964, incorporating body-on-frame construction using a 115-inch frame tied together with four crossmembers. The F-85/Cutlass (which had been a compact car on the Y-Body platform that debuted in 1961) became an intermediate model for 1964. It sat on the new A-Body platform, growing 11 inches in overall length.

As was the practice at the time, there was no shortage of model levels available within a single nameplate. The F-85 is a good example; it could be ordered in either Standard or Deluxe trim. There was also the top-of-the-heap F-85 Cutlass, which was similar to the Deluxe with upscale appointments.

Different body types were within each model level. The standard F-85 had three types: a two-door Club Coupe, a four-door sedan, and a four-door station wagon. The next rung up the ladder was the F-85 Deluxe, which had three flavors: a two-door Sport Coupe, a four-door sedan, and a four-door station wagon. At the top of the F-85 heap in 1964 was the F-85 Cutlass, which was available in a trio of styles: a two-door Coupe, a two-door Holiday Coupe, and a two-door convertible. It was quite a stew—and that was just the F-85 line. Oldsmobile had a full range of vehicles from the midsize F-85 to the gargantuan Ninety-Eight.

1964

GM's corporate policy in 1964 decreed that no engine larger than 330 ci could be used in the new A-Body platform. Detroit's Big Three automakers had been slugging it out on racetracks for years in an effort to "Win on Sunday, Sell on Monday." The money spent on these campaigns was considerable.

The tragic Le Mans crash in 1955 prompted the Automobile Manufacturers Association (AMA) to issue a ban to keep manufacturers from directly participating in racing. GM's president in 1957, Harlow Curtice, recommended that performance be de-emphasized. That didn't exactly put the brakes on factory involvement; it just adopted a lower profile. However, when John F. Kennedy became President in 1960, he brought his brother Robert to Washington as attorney general.

Robert Kennedy aimed his sights on General Motors, which was the largest corporation in the world at the time. Whispers of antitrust violations were in the air, and General Motors issued a statement in early 1963 that effectively ended the company's involvement in organized competition. At least that's what was presented to the world. General Motors wanted to have it all: winning races and mollifying the government. So, the automaker issued the internal directive regarding how many cubic inches could fit into a particular-sized vehicle.

This is the same policy that DeLorean ignored. Oldsmobile didn't want to drag out the 394-ci Rocket engine; it was a thick-wall design and was very heavy. Oldsmobile Marketing Executive David Jarrard felt that the intended GTO fighter required a minimum of 300 hp, so Oldsmobile engineering was tasked with getting the desired power into a lighter package.

Oldsmobile labeled every V-8 that it built from 1948 to 1990 as a *Rocket V-8*. Some years it was a Rocker 88, a Super Rocket, or a Jetfire Rocket, but Oldsmobile owned the Rocket nomenclature. All Rocket V-8s used a 90-degree bank angle and were built in Oldsmobile plants in Lansing, Michigan. The well-engineered 303-ci Rocket engine in the 1953 Oldsmobile 88 is considered by some to be the first muscle car.

As the 1950s passed, the displacement of the engine grew from 324 ci in 1954 to 371 ci in 1957. In 1957 and 1958, that engine could be had with a trio of 2-barrel carburetors, a package known as J2. Oldsmobile engineers knew performance. The problem was getting it into the showrooms. By the time the Pontiac crew slipped the GTO past the suits and into the showroom for 1964, Oldsmobiles had a new V-8 Generation 2 engine that displaced 330 ci.

The 330-ci engine was an interesting blend of old and new technology. The bore spacing and crank-to-cam distance was carried over from older engines, allowing Oldsmobile to use existing tooling. New to the engine was the iron block, cylinder heads, internal parts, and manifold castings. The cylinder stroke was a constant in Oldsmobile small-block engines at 3.385 inches. This engine used that stroke for its entire run, which ended production in 1990.

GTO-fighting duty fell to the new Generation 2 330-ci carbureted Jetfire Rocket V-8 fitted with a hotter hydraulic camshaft profile (278/282 duration intake/exhaust and 0.430/0.432 lift intake/exhaust) and beefed-up valve gear, including 1.875-inch intake valves and 1.562-inch exhaust valves. In this application, the cylinder bore was 3.938 inches.

Both small- and big-block Oldsmobile engines used identical bore centers, the difference being the deck height. Big-block engines used a small bore and long stroke to achieve the displacement. This was Oldsmobile's second small-block engine, which replaced the 215-ci V-8 in 1964. In 4-4-2 tune, the 330-ci engine's compression was 10.25:1. With the Rochester 4-GC 4-barrel carburetor under a dual-snorkel air cleaner, the engine was rated at 310 hp at 5,200 rpm and 360 ft-lbs of torque at 3,600 rpm.

Quality rotating components were used, including a forged-steel crankshaft, forged-steel connecting rods, and cast-aluminum pistons. Ahead of its time, the engine used a 6-degree valve angle, which created a wedge head configuration with a combustion chamber that burned very efficiently—so much so that it met emissions standards with a carburetor until 1990.

RPO B09

As time was short, the Oldsmobile engineers concentrated their efforts on improving handling. On the shelf were two heavy-duty engine/suspension packages aimed at law-enforcement vehicles: the RPO B01 City Cruiser Apprehender package and the RPO B07 Highway Patrol Apprehender. A combination of the two was created and called RPO B09, but it was marketed as the 4-4-2.

Priced at $136 when installed on the Cutlass and $285 when fitted to the F-85, the option slipped onto the order form in the summer of 1964. Documents from the period indicate that approximately 10 four-door sedans were fitted with the B09 package; talk about a sleeper!

Oldsmobile prided itself on the handling manners of the new 4-4-2, which were achieved by fitting heavy-duty 410-pound springs on the front and 160-pound springs in the rear. Front and rear stabilizer bars were included, and they did wonders for keeping the vehicle from heeling over in sharp turns. Brakes were in line with the times, which meant drums on all four wheels. It was a good idea to look *far* down the road. The emphasis was on *go* rather than *whoa*.

What Does It Stand For?

When originally released, the 4-4-2 moniker stood for 4-barrel (4), 4-speed (4), and dual exhaust (2). As the years went by, 4-4-2 morphed into meaning different aspects of the car, but one constant was well-rounded performance. In its freshman year, the muscular Oldsmobile A-Body was a hit.

Knowing Its Role

Performance was spirited for its time, and Oldsmobile, long known for engineering prowess, showed that it could also deliver the goods in a time crunch. The 3,440-pound 4-4-2 delivered a 0–60 time of 7.5 seconds for *MotorTrend* magazine and covered the quarter-mile in 15.5 seconds at 90 mph. The test car was fitted with a 3.55:1 rear axle ratio, the standard gearset was 3.36:1, and the top speed was 116 mph.

The 4-4-2 option (B09) could be ordered for any model F-85/Cutlass except the station wagon. It's a pity because that would have been a great grocery-getter. Considering the late release date of the 4-4-2, it's a wonder that Oldsmobile sold 2,999 units. Yet the division had dipped its toe in the super car market (as the segment was known at the time), and it was clear that this genre had some legs. The team at Oldsmobile had more in the pipeline—more power, more styling, and more presence. Bringing it to market took time, but the results were worth it.

The leadership at Oldsmobile had a tightrope to walk, as the brash DeLorean flouted company rules and built the Pontiac GTO. As the middle rung on the GM ladder of status (Chevrolet at the bottom, then Pontiac, Oldsmobile, Buick, and Cadillac at the top), Oldsmobile was a sure bet for stylish, reliable, well-engineered automobiles that were perfect for a rising middle-level manager. But performance? Leave that for those brash lead-foots at Chevy or maybe Pontiac.

However, Oldsmobile didn't lose sight of its competition history as it released the 4-4-2. One of the risks that Pontiac created was that it became a target, not just for Ford and Chrysler, but for the other GM divisions. There were plenty of people at Oldsmobile who cut their teeth helping the division win big on racetracks, and when the call came from Oldsmobile headquarters that an effective foil to the GTO was needed, they rose to the occasion.

How to Market

From its inception, the 4-4-2 was to personify an executive express. Oldsmobile, lacking a perceived performance background, just didn't know how to market the 1964 4-4-2. This segment in the marketplace was new to everyone, and Oldsmobile was caught without an effective marketing strategy to counter the Pontiac effort.

Oldsmobile advertisements for the period were simple, quickly produced pieces that put the 4-4-2 name in print but were visually boring. This was new ground for everyone, and Oldsmobile, with its marketing emphasis on sophisticated automobiles for discerning buyers, had to shift gears and start chasing a new breed of buyers.

Pontiac had the youth market in its sights and, from the GTO's debut, aggressively targeted the young and young at heart. Oldsmobile tended to push the new 4-4-2 toward the buyer who was looking for a police interceptor that civilians could drive. At Oldsmobile, advertisements boasted, "Police needed it . . . Olds built it . . .

Pursuit proved it! Put this one on your WANTED list!" Heart be still.

Oldsmobile couldn't say that the new 4-4-2 was faster than the GTO. The Pontiac's 389-ci V-8 cranked out 325 hp, while the new 4-4-2 was marketed as having 310 hp. However, Oldsmobile enjoyed the perks that went along with being a GM division a step up the ladder from Pontiac: better quality interior materials, superior ride and handling, and, for model year 1964, exclusivity.

The 4-4-2 was eventually dubbed the *banker's express*, and this was an accurate moniker. Oldsmobiles were never inexpensive vehicles, and the 4-4-2 was a way to expand into new markets and lighten customers' wallets. Oldsmobile buyers got a lot of bang for their buck, and that trend continued into 1965. The engineers at Oldsmobile were filling the pipeline with impressive products, and soon the fledgling performance battles erupted into all-out war.

1965

Executives at Oldsmobile had high hopes for the newish 4-4-2, but the man who had green-lighted the project had to leave the division. Jack Wolfram had been fighting health concerns since late 1961, and by 1964, it was clear that a successor was needed. Harold N. Metzel took over as Oldsmobile's general manager on July 6, 1964.

Metzel's background as chief engineer came in handy, as the performance wars were heating up. Having a leader

It's hard to believe that the Cutlass in 1966 was considered an intermediate vehicle. With a trunk as big as the engine compartment, a family could take a multiweek summer vacation with room for plenty of souvenirs. The 4-4-2's beefy powerplant effortlessly flattened hills.

Hurst was the pick of the performance shifters, and Oldsmobile ensured that the 4-4-2 was equipped with it. Chevrolet used the Muncie, which was famous for jamming between gears and being difficult to know which gear you were in. The Hurst shifters didn't suffer from these ills, and they were considered mandatory in real performance cars.

who understood performance and how to make it was invaluable. Replacing Metzel in the chief engineer slot was John Beltz.

More Cubic Inches, Please!

The market for performance cars was starting to boil, and Oldsmobile was well placed to boost its 4-4-2 deep into the competitive fray. The mantra across all manufacturers was *better living with cubic inches*, and Oldsmobile had plenty of experience with big engines.

General Motors realized that bigger displacement engines were the immediate future, as Ford and Chrysler were slipping beefier powerplants beneath their hoods. A GM corporate edit limiting displacement to 400 ci worked in Oldsmobile's favor, as the writing was on the wall: go big or go home.

400 Stage II Rocket

On the menu of Oldsmobile engines for 1965 was a new entry: the Stage II Rocket, which displaced 425 ci. Oldsmobile engineers reduced the bore of the new iron-block engine from 4.125 inches to 4.00, the bore was 3.975 inches, and the resulting powerplant displaced 400 ci. Viola! Into the 4-4-2 it went.

This optional 400-ci RPO L69 engine was rated at 360 hp and 440 ft-lbs of torque, thanks in part to its three Rochester 2GC 2-barrel carburetors. It was priced at $264.54. When equipped with a hotter camshaft and flexible tubing that fed cool air to the air-cleaner housing, it had a W-30.

Each GM division painted its engines with a unique color. This was a period when the divisions fought each other as hard as they fought Ford or Chrysler. The GM divisions behaved as if they were separate companies. In the 1970s, General Motors started to install a single engine in a wide range of divisional vehicles in an effort to cut costs.

Now, 4-4-2 stood for 400 ci (4); 4-barrel, 700-cfm Rochester 4CG Quadrajet carburetor (4); and dual exhaust (2). To no one's surprise, power was up from the year before. It was rated at 345 hp at 4,500 rpm and a tire-shredding 440 ft-lbs of torque at just 3,200 rpm. With its 10.25:1 compression ratio, the use of Sunoco 260 was strongly suggested.

Hydraulic lifters kept the owner from setting valve lash on the weekend as well as dampening noise. Another feature that kept sound from the engine compartment down was the cooling fan. It was designed to not exceed 4,000 rpm, and it developed maximum airflow at just 3,300 rpm. Engine internals were strong: a forged crankshaft and forged connecting rods were standard. On the drag strip, the upgrade to more cubic inches paid off. Eric Dahlquist of *Hot Rod* magazine saw the quarter-mile flash by in the 15-second range with a 95-mph trap speed, which was very credible for a vehicle of this size.

Handle with Care

The beefy engine was surrounded by a score of heavy-duty components from the frame to the mufflers. Even the motor mounts and driveshaft were pulled from the heavy-duty bin. With its heavy-duty suspension, the 4-4-2 enjoyed a trait that many of its competitors lacked: the ability to tackle a winding road with confidence. Stabilizer bars at both ends were huge (about 1 inch in diameter) and made of SAE 1070 steel. They helped reduce the tendency of a 3,600-pound vehicle to heel over like a sailboat in a storm.

Many transmission choices were available. A three-on-the-column was standard. Optional setups included a 3-speed with Hurst floor shifter or a 4-speed close-ratio floor shifter with a Muncie transmission. Drivers wanting to go the automatic route had one choice: the 2-speed Jetaway automatic.

With its strong horizontal lines, 115-inch wheelbase, and imposing proportions, the 1966 4-4-2 oozed attitude. The narrow 7.34x14-inch bias-ply tires didn't stand a chance of getting all of the power down.

Aesthetics

Mild changes to the body gave the 1965 4-4-2 more in the way of exterior badging. The front grille was cleaned up with a single horizontal bar spanning the width of the opening. Blacked-out trim behind the bar enhanced the brightwork and gave the impression of muscular width. In front of the rear wheels below the rear windows were faux vents, which were meant to suggest rear brake cooling. It was an affordable nod to sportiness.

Discreet badging in the early years of the 4-4-2 was tasteful, as seen on the rear of this 1966 model.

Fitted with dog-dish hubcaps, it's clear that the original buyer put his money under the hood. The rear anti-sway bar is visible beneath the differential. It did a good job of reining in body roll under heavy cornering. The vents in the front fenders were nonfunctional, but they looked good.

The Cutlass line received a mild freshening for 1966, and the 4-4-2 benefited from the massaged sheet metal. Quad headlights and a bar bisecting the grille gave the 4-4-2 a strong face. Within the grille was the unique 4-4-2 tri-color emblem. This vehicle is an example of a post car, meaning it had a rigid B-pillar, giving the body considerable structural stiffness.

When it came to shifting gears in a performance car in the 1960s, there was only one name that could do the job with precision and reliability: Hurst. Pontiac insisted that its GTO be equipped with the famed shifter, and Oldsmobile followed suit with the 4-4-2. So powerful was the Hurst image that Oldsmobile mounted this callout on the trunk lid.

Comfort was key in the GM A-Body offerings, and the Oldsmobile Cutlass 4-4-2 was no exception. With room for six adults, the interior was a tasteful mix of colors and textures. This 1966 car is equipped with a 4-speed manual transmission, which might cause some discomfort with a center passenger.

Oldsmobile carried the horizontal quad headlight treatment over from 1965 into the freshened body for 1966. The 4-4-2's broad shoulders were evident in this view, giving the Oldsmobile a menacing visage. Spanning a width of 75.4 inches, it would fill a lane.

The Cutlass showed off new lines in 1966 with crisp fender creases running fore and aft. The slight kick-up plate just behind the doors broke up the vast expanse of sheet metal. The stance on this 1966 example says muscle car like no other.

Getting Its Ad Together

One thing that wasn't cooling was Oldsmobile's marketing for the 4-4-2. For the 1964 model year, Oldsmobile used black-and-white ads that did nothing to convey any sense of automotive adventure. These ads were an effective cure for insomnia. In Oldsmobile's defense, it was now chasing a market segment with which the division had little experience and was evolving from day to day: the youth market.

Oldsmobile had been comfortable for decades as a provider of vehicles for upwardly mobile white-collar buyers. Suddenly, it was thrust into building, marketing, and selling a performance vehicle for the young and the young at heart. It took the division time to dial in its marketing efforts, but it eventually created a unique marketing campaign that clearly set Oldsmobile apart from its competition. Stay tuned.

W-29

The 4-4-2 option was officially listed as W-29, which was a practice that carried through to 1967. This was

New package
of instant action:
Olds 4 4 2

What's the 4-4-2? Just the sweetest piece of live action on wheels! Small wonder, too, when you check its credentials. An all-new, all-its-own 400-cubic-inch V-8. Four-barrel carb. Twin pipes. Heavy-duty suspension. Nylon red-line tires. Three smooth transmission availabilities: 3-speed synchromesh, close-ratio 4-on-the-floor or Jetaway automatic. You can tuck all this "instant action" into any F-85 V-8 coupe or convertible. And 4-4-2 prices start below any other high-performance car in America designed for every-day driving. Sound like your kind of action? See your Oldsmobile Dealer. He has your number: 4-4-2! Oldsmobile Division • General Motors Corp.

'65 OLDSMOBILE
The Rocket Action Car!

Photographed in a studio, this advertisement for the 1965 Oldsmobile 4-4-2 pointed out that the vehicle came equipped with a raft of performance items mandatory for a muscle car. The sentence in italics says it all: "And 4-4-2 prices start below any other high-performance car in America designed for everyday driving." Oldsmobile was implying that you could have it all: blistering performance and practicality. (Photo Courtesy General Motors)

If you've got the cap...

Olds has the car!

A digger's dream, this 4-4-2! Here storms a lean 'n' mean Rocket V-8 . . . 400 cubes, 345 horses, quad pots. Goodies like twin acoustically tuned, chambered pipes . . . heavy-duty shocks, front and rear stabilizers and 4 coil springs. Result: unique 4-4-2 action and road sense. How many cents? *Lowest priced high-performance car in America designed for everyday driving!* This woolly machine waits for you at your Oldsmobile Dealer's now. *Hurry!*

'65 OLDSMOBILE

Try a Rocket in Action . . .
Look to __Olds__ for the __New__!

Olds **442** was here!

442 Lowest priced high-performance car in America!

OLDSMOBILE DIVISION • GENERAL MOTORS CORPORATION

Action-ready equipment includes: 400-cu.-in., 345-h.p. V-8 • 4-barrel carb • Acoustically tuned, chambered twin pipes • Heavy-duty frame • Heavy-duty springs and shocks • Heavy-duty suspension • Front and rear stabilizers • Nylon red-line tires • Three transmission availabilities — 3-speed synchromesh, 4-on-the-floor, Jetaway automatic — with action-matched axles! Ask for it by number: 4-4-2 . . . in any F-85 V-8 coupe or convertible.

'65 OLDSMOBILE

Try a Rocket in Action...Look to Olds for the New!

Implied performance was the key to this advertisement for the 1965 Oldsmobile 4-4-2. It was not an expensive ad to create, as Oldsmobile was still hedging its bets on the longevity of the performance car craze. It didn't take long for the division to realize that there was serious money to be made selling muscle cars. (Photo Courtesy General Motors)

The advertising agency that created this spot for the 1965 4-4-2 hadn't received word that the 1960s performance cars were targeted at the young and the young at heart. The cap was intended to evoke driving sporty English cars, not fire-breathing, tire-melting, straight-line missiles. (Photo Courtesy General Motors)

the first time that Oldsmobile used the W-code but certainly not the last. In prior years, Oldsmobile labeled its performance packages with a *J*, but the leadership at Oldsmobile wanted something different. John Beltz had a close working relationship with Jack "Doc" Watson, a performance guru who worked for Hurst but wore a lot of different hats. Watson assisted Beltz in the development of many of the components that comprised various Oldsmobile W packages. Beltz decided to label these as *W*, saying that would remind him of Watson.

Oldsmobile was selling a real performance car—just not quickly enough. It was a good sophomore year performance for the muscular Oldsmobiles, but taken in a broader context, the division knew that there was heavy lifting to be done.

Unfortunately for Oldsmobile, Pontiac's GTO was kicking Oldsmobile's tail in the all-important sales tally. The Tri-Power carburetor induction system that Pontiac offered in the GTO was a huge seller. The division sold 20,547 Tri-Power-equipped cars out of 75,352 total GTO sales in 1965. Oldsmobile sold a total of 25,003 4-4-2s in the same time frame. It was decided at Oldsmobile that its experience in multiple carburation would be tapped to bring more grunt to the party.

1966: The Path to Power via Fresh Air

There was a period of time when General Motors didn't hang on to a body design for a decade. In the late 1950s, Chevrolet was introducing a new body shell every year. By the 1960s, a vehicle was showing its styling age within two to three years. General Motors had a new A-Body platform that all of its divisions (except Cadillac) would massage for the 1966 model year.

Oldsmobile wanted to stay fresh, and for 1966, it

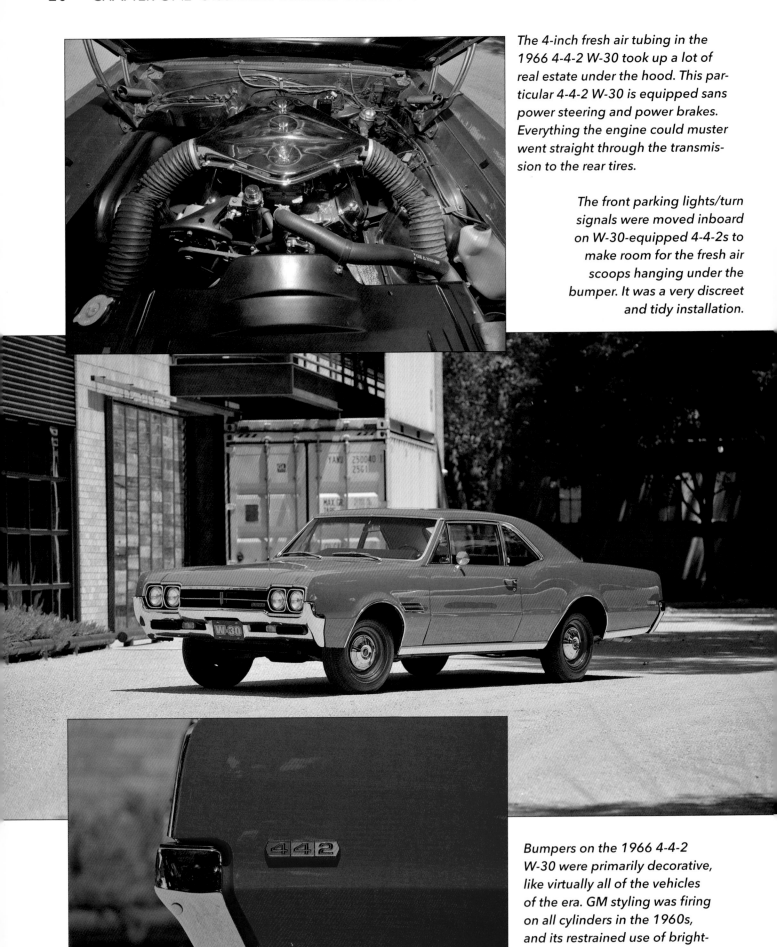

The 4-inch fresh air tubing in the 1966 4-4-2 W-30 took up a lot of real estate under the hood. This particular 4-4-2 W-30 is equipped sans power steering and power brakes. Everything the engine could muster went straight through the transmission to the rear tires.

The front parking lights/turn signals were moved inboard on W-30-equipped 4-4-2s to make room for the fresh air scoops hanging under the bumper. It was a very discreet and tidy installation.

Bumpers on the 1966 4-4-2 W-30 were primarily decorative, like virtually all of the vehicles of the era. GM styling was firing on all cylinders in the 1960s, and its restrained use of brightwork was impressive.

used the Cutlass to show off a new crisp look. Bill Mitchell was calling the shots in GM styling, and his hand was visible in the entire GM portfolio but especially in performance cars, such as the Corvette, the Buick Riviera, and the A-Body vehicles. The front-end treatment was immediately reminiscent of the 1965 model with the four headlights, single horizontal bar, and leading-edge hood treatment. But aft of that, new knife-edge fender lines flowed into handsome vertical taillights.

The Cutlass was an A-Body midsize automobile, but understand that it was a seriously good-sized vehicle. It rode on a 117-inch wheelbase, and its overall length was 204.2 inches. Compare that to a full-size 1966 Cadillac Sedan de Ville, which had a wheelbase of 129.5 inches and an overall length of 224 inches. No matter how you slice it, *midsize* in GM parlance was a garage-filling car. Buyers had three body configurations from which to choose: a two-door coupe, a convertible, and a two-door sedan (post).

With its dog-dish hubcaps and painted blue roof, this 1966 F-85 Club Coupe could (at first glance) be mistaken for a bland commuter car. However, the subtle badge in the grille and the dual intake scoops nestled in the front bumper hint at the vehicle's true purpose: making the local tire dealer rich.

This 1966 4-4-2 W-30 was intended for fair-weather racing, period. Devoid of both a radio and climate controls, it was stripped to its essentials. A front bench seat was standard on entry-level cars.

Beneath the Hurst shifter in the 1966 W-30 was a 4-speed Muncie transmission. At the other end of the driveshaft was a set of 4.11:1 Posi gears in a 12-bolt rear end.

Full wheel covers were an option in 1966, and this 4-4-2 W-30 originally came with these dog-dish, or "poverty," hubcaps. The stylish vents on the front fenders were for looks only.

There was plenty of room to spread out in a GM A-Body in 1966. Not lavishly appointed but comfortable, this 4-4-2 W-30 was intended for one purpose: blurring the scenery. Only 54 W-30 packages were installed at the factory; 93 were bolted on at dealerships.

The mesh pattern in the middle of the dashboard was the screen for the AM radio speaker. The front seat backs pivoted forward for access to the roomy back seat. On a hot day, the vinyl upholstery could get a bit uncomfortable.

Looking more like an afterthought than anything else, the tachometer on the 1966 4-4-2 W-30 was squeezed onto the edge of the dashboard. It wasn't the best location for such a critical instrument, but at least it had one.

Power Up!

Under the bold exterior, Oldsmobile engineers fitted more power. By 1966, all of the Detroit automakers were engaged in a no-holds-barred war in the muscle car segment, or, as they were called at the time, *super cars*. The RPO L78 400-ci V-8 still held court at Oldsmobile and was the standard engine in the 4-4-2. Using a single 4-barrel Quadrajet carburetor, it was rated at 350 hp, a 5-hp increase attributable to a slight bump up in compression to 10.5:1. Transmission choices were carried over from 1965.

For buyers who wanted yet more, there was an optional engine (RPO L69), which was offered late in the 1966 build cycle. It consisted of an induction system to make your mouth water: a trio of 2-barrel Carter carbs atop a special intake manifold using a progressive mechanical linkage.

Many people believe that Oldsmobile copied Pontiac's GTO in the area of multiple carburetors. However, truth be told, it was more like Pontiac copied Oldsmobile. In 1957, Oldsmobile produced a triple-carburetor setup for its J2 Power Pack option fitted to its 371-ci

One of the rare 1966 4-4-2 Track Pack vehicles, this car was equipped with the potent L69 400-ci engine rated at 360 hp. Atop the big-block was a trio of Rochester 2-barrel carburetors hidden beneath the W-30 dual-snorkel air cleaner. Inside the blueprinted block was a camshaft with an aggressive 308 degrees of duration and 0.474-inch lift for both intake and exhaust valves. In reality, horsepower was nearly 400.

Rocket engine. The system had been guided to production by Pete Estes, who was the assistant chief engineer at Oldsmobile before he was poached by Pontiac as chief engineer in September 1956.

The J2 package was used until the end of 1958 and then pulled from production. However, the knowledge gained at Oldsmobile was put back into use in 1966 with the 4-4-2 RPO L69.

The L69 retained the strong 400-ci block. The V-code heads (the *T* stamped on them denoted Tri-Carb) used L69-specfic stronger valve springs. In the heads were

Model year 1966 saw Oldsmobile advertise the 4-4-2 as a full-spectrum performance car that was capable of delivering sparkling straight-line acceleration as well as confidence-inspiring handling. The style of the ad itself was rather old school, but with the D. P. Brother Co. ad agency about to be snapped up by Leo Burnett Co., the tone of Oldsmobile's ad campaigns was about to change for the better. (Photo Courtesy General Motors)

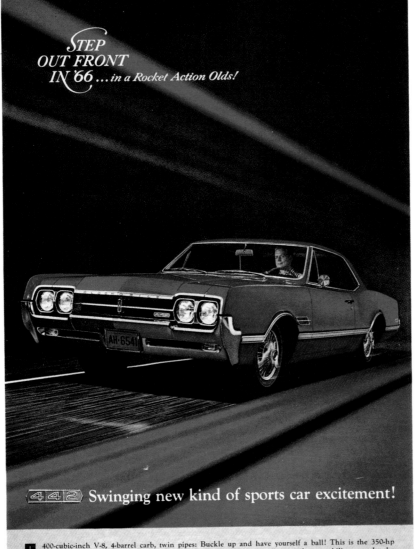

STEP OUT FRONT IN '66 ...in a Rocket Action Olds!

442 Swinging new kind of sports car excitement!

400-cubic-inch V-8, 4-barrel carb, twin pipes: Buckle up and have yourself a ball! This is the 350-hp 4-4-2. With heavy-duty suspension, built to K.O. the roughest roads. Front and rear stabilizers to take the "bend" out of curves, the bind out of corners. And under it all—pavement-biting red-line tires! But the swinging-est thing about Olds 4-4-2 is its surprisingly modest price!   LOOK TO OLDS FOR THE NEW!
Oldsmobile Division • General Motors Corp.

Advertising agency D. P. Brother Co., based in Detroit, handled the Oldsmobile account for decades. Muscle cars were a new field for the established firm, and its approach to advertising the genre was very conservative. The photography in this ad for the 1966 4-4-2 was created by the legendary Boulevard Photographic of Detroit, Michigan. (Photo Courtesy General Motors)

With a pair of flexible tubes that looked as if they belonged on the back of a clothes dryer, the air-cleaner assembly in the 1966 4-4-2 W-30 was filled with ambient air pulled in from a pair of scoops beneath the front bumper under the headlights. The installation of the tubing required that the battery be mounted outside of the engine compartment.

2.067/1.629-inch valves and 1.6:1 rocker arms.

The camshaft was hotter than the one found in the L78. It had a hydraulic lifter cam, as did the L78s. But the L69's cam used a 308-degree duration with 82-degree overlap, whereas the L78 cam was a 278-degree affair. Power output for public consumption was 360 hp at 5,000 rpm, while torque was listed at 440 ft-lbs at 3,600 rpm.

Three Rochester 2GV 2-barrel carburetors sat atop a cast-iron intake manifold that incorporated a pair of block-off plates flanking the center carb. These plates allowed the driver to open or shut the heat riser: open for street use or closed for drag-strip action. Unlike Pontiac's

approach to a tri-power setup, Oldsmobile used a mechanical linkage to open the front and rear carburetors. Nailing the throttle in the GTO allowed engine vacuum to swing the secondary carbs open, swelling engine output accordingly. Oldsmobile's approach gave an entirely different feel at full throttle. Mashing the gas pedal to the floor dumped a *lot* of fuel into the engine, slamming the driver into the seat. Horsepower was rated at 360, which was the same as the GTO. Bragging rights among owners was important, and big power numbers sold cars.

Beneath the car, Oldsmobile engineers worked to give the 4-4-2 an edge in handling compared to its performance competitors. The ride was firm but not harsh, controlled but not floaty. The 4-4-2 was the poster car for the gentleman's express.

In its June 1966 issue, *MotorTrend* magazine's John Ethridge summed up his time with the 4-4-2 L69: "If the 4-4-2 doesn't do all the things you want a car to do, you need more than one car. We would be hard put to find another car that does so many things so well."

Oldsmobile bolted together 2,129 L69-equipped 4-4-2s for 1966.

RPO W-30

But wait, there's more! Oldsmobile was getting tired of the 4-4-2 getting kicked around by its arch-rival, the Pontiac GTO. The sales disparity of the two bruisers in 1966 was alarming: Pontiac unloaded 96,496 GTOs, while Oldsmobile sold 21,997 4-4-2s. Something had to be done. John Beltz tasked his crew to design a package that could not only match or beat the GTO in a straight line but also handle well, which was something that most

Because the fresh-air ducting of the W-30 induction system required so much real estate under the hood, the battery was relocated to the passenger's side of the trunk. This had the beneficial effect of moving a hefty amount of weight rearward, improving traction. However, this location prevented the W-30 option from being offered in convertibles, as the folded top stack sat where the battery was located. Thus, Oldsmobile didn't offer the W-30 option on a ragtop 4-4-2 in 1966.

performance cars of the era had serious trouble doing.

Beltz wanted an option that would transform the 4-4-2 from an elegantly muscular contender to a brutal bully dressed in a suit. The result was RPO W-30 Fresh Air Induction System. However, it was so much more than just an unconventional induction system.

Oldsmobile Special Projects Manager Dale Smith had been in touch with drag racers for years, and the wealth of advice and requests he had was put into reality with the W-30 option. Attention to detail was not overlooked; the trunk-mounted battery placement is an example.

RPO W-30 was announced in May 1966, and it started finding its way under hoods in the second week of June 1966. Officially called Outside Air Induction, it used a pair of 4-inch-diameter flexible tubes to feed cool, ambient air from the grille into a special air cleaner. The inlets

for the tubes were located where the front turn signals were fitted, requiring the lights to be moved inboard of the scoops.

Because the flex tubes took up so much real estate under the hood, the battery was relocated to the trunk, where it sat above the rear axle on the passenger's side so that its heft would help balance out the driver's weight. The battery placement was in the location that convertible 4-4-2s used to stow a lowered top. So, rather than move the battery again, Oldsmobile simply made the W-30 option unavailable in the ragtop.

NHRA Homologation

Oldsmobile rated the W-30 at 360 hp, which was the same as the regular L69 engine. At speed with the big tubes feeding cool air to the 400-ci V-8, it made 360

In 1966, the 4-4-2 was kicking tail on the quarter-mile in the Stock Eliminator class, led by the fierce Track Pack option. The factory built just 54 of the stormers. Demand for more led Oldsmobile to ship the parts needed for the conversion to its dealers for installation. A total of 93 4-4-2s were retrofitted with the package, including this example originally sold at Bob McDonald Chevrolet Oldsmobile in Halifax, Nova Scotia, Canada.

The dual intake scoops for the W-30 option can be seen in the bumper, just outboard of the parking lights. Feeding the cool ambient air to the engine made a noticeable difference in performance, especially at high speed. The location of the scoops allowed undisturbed air to be fed to the induction system.

Most 1966 4-4-2 W-30 Track Pack cars led harsh lives a quarter-mile at a time. Owner-installed headers can be seen glinting under the car. Slicks didn't have much of a chance against the beefy torque that the big Oldsmobile 400 churned out. The B-pillar on the F-85 Club Coupe bodystyle provided additional rigidity, a desired trait in a drag car.

Looking like a car that Grandma would take to the grocery store, this 1966 4-4-2 W-30 Track Pack beast came with a couple of features that Grandma might question, such as the tall 4-speed shifter and tiny tachometer to the left of the dashboard. The lack of a radio wouldn't put a smile on her face, either.

hp. However, the L69 was underrated. It was a beast. Coming into production as late in the model year as it did, Oldsmobile only built 54 from the factory.

For the W-30 to qualify for National Hot Rod Association (NHRA) racing, a minimum of 50 had to be homologated. The track-driven cars were successful on the track, and quickly put the words *Oldsmobile* and *performance* on everyone's lips. The immediate success of the W-30 in the quarter-mile sent Oldsmobile drivers racing to their dealership's parts counters, where the pieces to build your own W-30 were available under the label *Track Pack*.

When the model year closed, a total of 93 Track Pack W-30s were finished. Total 4-4-2 production for model year 1966 was 21,997 units.

The 4-4-2 W-30 showed the public what Oldsmobile could bring to the performance car arena. In stock form, a W-30 could lunge down the drag strip in 13.8 seconds at 103 mph. Those were serious numbers in the super car field, and it was clear that Oldsmobile had more in the pipeline. Everyone was looking to see what 1967 would bring.

The forward carburetor of the three on top of a 1966 4-4-2 W-30 Track Pack 400-ci engine is shown. Under full throttle, all six barrels of the induction system pushed a lot of fuel into the intake manifold, giving the driver an explosive kick in the pants. To hasten throttle response, the outboard carbs used a mechanical linkage (rather than vacuum) to open. The combustion chambers displaced 75 cc.

On the drag strip, the biggest problem that a driver of a 1966 4-4-2 W-30 Track Pack car had was trying to get these slicks to hook up and launch the car without wheelspin. This particular car tore up drag strips across Eastern Canada.

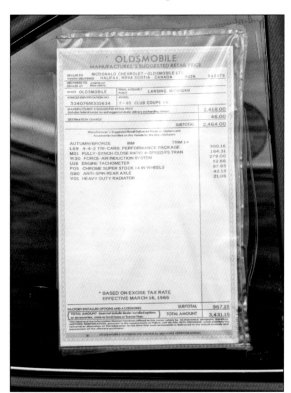

This 1966 4-4-2 was optioned out for one purpose: competition. Fewer options meant less weight. It was one of 93 vehicles converted to a Track Pack car by an Oldsmobile dealer.

Virtually all GM vehicles built in the 1960s rolled down the assembly line with this tag attached to the cowl early in the build process. This allowed line workers to tell at a glance what significant options with which this particular car would be equipped. The LAN code denotes location of assembly. In this case, it's the Lansing, Michigan, Oldsmobile plant.

The *W* stood for *Wow!*

A new level of luxury was introduced in the F-85/Cutlass lineup for 1966, the Cutlass Supreme, which was the starting point for all 4-4-2s built that year. This arrangement continued into the 1967 model year. Five versions were available: two-door Sport Coupe, two-door convertible, four-door Town Sedan, two-door Holiday hardtop, and four-door Holiday hardtop. Only two-door models were eligible for 4-4-2 status.

Model year 1967 didn't see many exterior changes with the 4-4-2. The most prominent was a one-year-only functional louvered hood. Under the huge hood were more changes. The most pronounced was the departure of the Tri-Carb option.

For the 1967 model year, the 4-4-2 sported a new headlight treatment. It still used a horizontal quad-bulb configuration, but now the lights were separated by the parking lights. On W-30 models, the area above and beneath the parking-light lens was converted into the scoops feeding cool air to the air cleaner via a pair of flexible tubes.

Oldsmobile sold 24,829 4-4-2s in 1967, but just 337 Hardtop Coupe 4-4-2 W-30s were sold in that model year. The 4-4-2 option was only available on the Cutlass Supreme in 1967.

As only Cutlass Supremes were the basis for 4-4-2s in 1967, the car still wore its CS badge on the trunk lid at the keyhole. The backup lights were integral in the rear bumper, flanking the license plate.

GM executives were taken aback by Oldsmobile and Pontiac's fitment of triple carburetors on a number of vehicles in 1966, and GM President Ed Cole was firm that multiple carburetors were to be fitted to only two vehicles: the Corvette and the Corvair. Oldsmobile followed the corporate edict by sticking with a single 4-barrel carburetor in the 1967 4-4-2. A number of incremental improvements were slipped into the Oldsmobile A-Body for 1967, which resulted in a polished performance car.

For 1967, Oldsmobile mounted the tachometer within the center of the right-hand instrument cluster. It was difficult to read when rowing through the gears with gusto; it was better to shift by ear. The bucket seats were comfortable but didn't offer much lateral support, which was key in a car that could actually corner well.

Above and below the 1967 4-4-2 W-30's parking light housing were a pair of scoop inlets that fed ambient air into the air cleaner housing via a pair of flexible ducts. This was the only external clue that a 4-4-2 was a W-30-equipped car.

Riding on a 115-inch wheelbase, the 1967 4-4-2 W-30 gave a balanced ride, finding that sweet spot of road feel and comfort.

Oldsmobile affixed this decal onto the driver-side valve cover in the 1967 4-4-2, providing basic engine information with an attractive presentation. Lifting the hood on an impressive powerplant meant a lot.

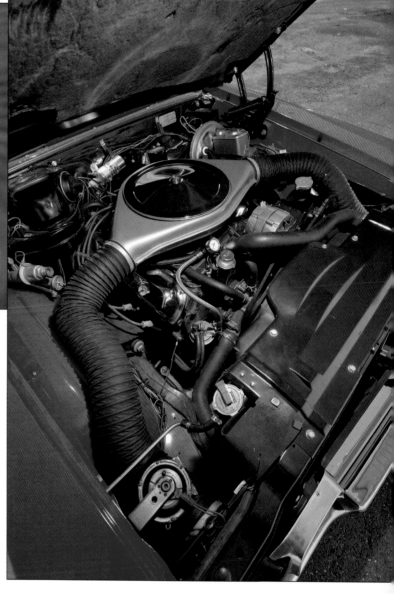

With the induction tubing running all over the engine compartment, Oldsmobile engineers located the car's dual horns on the edge of the fenders above the flex hoses. Oldsmobile built only 502 W-30s in 1967, making them one of the most capable and rare American muscle cars. With 385 hp under the long hood, it wasn't difficult to lay waste to the set of rear tires in a very short amount of time.

Shifting Gears

One of the more significant improvements was the departure of the 2-speed Jetaway automatic transmission. It was replaced on the option sheet by the 3-speed Turbo Hydra-matic automatic. Costing buyers $236.97, this transmission proved to be one of the finest automatics ever designed.

In the 4-4-2, the Hydra-matic was bolted to the same RPO L78 400-ci V-8 that had been used the previous year. The standard transmission in the 4-4-2 was a 3-speed manual with a floor-mounted shifter. Optional manual transmissions included the M20 and M21 4-speed boxes.

When the 4-4-2 for 1967 was ordered with the automatic transmission, the standard rear-axle gearset was 3.08:1. It wasn't a neck-snapping gear, but it was a good balance of acceleration and fuel economy. It also helped engine speed stay down on the highway. Cruising at 65 mph showed 3,000 rpm on the tachometer. Optional

gears included 3.55:1, 3.90:1, and a stump-pulling 4.33:1 fitted in a beefy 12-bolt housing.

A major trait of the 4-4-2 that carried forward into the new model year was the superb suspension. Using beefy anti-roll bars in the front and rear and wisely chosen spring rates, the 4-4-2 could deliver what few other American performance cars could in 1967: the ability to make its way around a corner without dragging a door handle.

Oldsmobile's chassis engineers dialed in the 4-4-2 to provide drivers with a reasonable amount of feedback. Front disc brakes made it onto the option sheet for 1967 and did wonders slowing the 3,850-pound 4-4-2 from highway speeds. Power was still provided by the 400-ci engine and 4-barrel carburetor combination that saw duty in 1966. It was rated at 350 hp at 5,000 rpm and 440 ft-lbs of torque at 3,600 rpm.

What did all this mechanical goodness mean on a drag strip? *Super Stock* magazine tested a 4-4-2 W-30 for

The top of the 1967 4-4-2 W-30 air cleaner had a removable lid that was held on by a wing nut, which allowed for the replacement of the paper air-cleaner element. In the 1960s, the appearance of the engine compartment, especially in performance cars, was as stylish as the exterior.

The 1967 4-4-2, which was the last year for the broad-shouldered look, received a light touch with the restyling brush. The wide grille, extending from front fender tip to front fender tip, exuded "Oldsmobile," and this familial design feature played across the Oldsmobile line as well into the 1968 redesign.

Hurst was still shifting gears in the 1967 4-4-2 as well as the W-30. The shifter ball fell readily to hand, and the beefy assembly slid into gear with a satisfying thunk. The center console was a $54 option. Cars magazine hurled a 1967 W-30 that was equipped with 4.33:1 gears down a drag strip and walked away with 14.1-second run at 103 mph. Not bad. Not bad at all.

Oldsmobile borrowed the Toronado name to back up the catchphrase Engineered for Excitement in this colorful advertisement for the 1967 Oldsmobile 4-4-2. Shot entirely in a studio, it placed models of the desired demographic doing activities that the advertising agency felt reflected the interests of potential buyers: playing guitar, creating artwork, and sitting in a topdown convertible with an open umbrella. Leather driving gloves were optional. (Photo Courtesy General Motors)

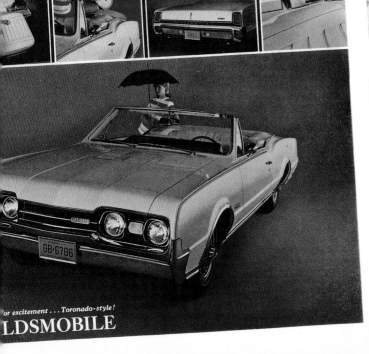

its August 1967 issue, and the results were impressive. With a third member filled with a 4.33:1 gearset and rowing a 4-speed manual transmission, the W-30 flashed across the lights in 13.99 seconds at 102.4 mph. That's a damn fast car.

Back for More

The W-30 option was alive and well for 1967. Granted, the triple-threat L69 option was gone, but the resourceful engineers at Oldsmobile continued to earn their paychecks by injecting horsepower beneath the hood. As in 1966, W-30-equipped cars used a pair of flexible tubes to feed cool air into the air cleaner; the inlet scoop was now mounted between the headlights.

While GM's A-Body architecture was shared with other divisions, Oldsmobile's take on a gentleman's express was especially handsome. Buick had the Skylark, Chevrolet had the Chevelle, and Pontiac had the GTO, but the 4-4-2 W-30 was an elegant bruiser.

Front disc brakes were standard on the 1967 4-4-2 W-30. Oldsmobile realized that with the abundance of go, attention had to be put on whoa. The five-spoke 14x7-inch styled steel wheels were popular and rugged.

The air cleaner housing was unique to 4-4-2 W-30s in 1967. Rare beyond belief today, they fetch serious sums of money, if you can find one at all.

Only factory 4-4-2 W-30s were equipped with red inner fender liners. Note the tidy routing of the flex tubing around the power brake booster and the power steering pump. There still wasn't room for the battery, so it was mounted in the trunk.

Once again, W-30s saw the battery mounted in the trunk due to the intrusion of the ducts in the engine compartment. A hotter 308-degree duration hydraulic camshaft was part of the W-30 package. W-30s had a *C* cast into the front of the driver-side head, which is a quick way to help identify a real W-30.

In its February 1967 issue, *MotorTrend* magazine wrung out a 4-4-2, posting a quarter-mile time of 15.5 seconds at 91 mph with two people in the car. This vehicle was equipped with an automatic transmission and the base 3.08:1 rear axle ratio.

Red Hot Inner Fenders

One item that was slipped into the engine compartment in 1967 was red injection-plastic inner fender liners. These liners were part of the W-30 package and replaced the metal fender liners. Originally developed by Pontiac material engineer Joshua Madden for the GTO, they were used on the 1967 4-4-2 W-30 as a vivid indicator that this was the top-dog Oldsmobile.

All of the performance vehicle manufacturers in 1967 were pitching their products to the increasingly potent youth market, and bright colors, splashy graphics, and unique features found their way into production in an effort to attract the young and young at heart.

Oldsmobile saw a modest increase in 4-4-2 production for 1967, as 24,829 were built (502 with the W-30 option). This was the final year of the first-generation 4-4-2, but Oldsmobile had a worthy successor in the wings that would take the 4-4-2 and W-30 to new levels.

Guide T3 headlights flank the 4-4-2 W-30's scoops on this 1967 vehicle. The headlights did a good job of lighting the road for the era, which is a nice way of saying they sucked at lighting the road. In a performance car, such as the 4-4-2 W-30, it didn't take a lot of throttle to overdrive the lights at night.

For model year 1967, Oldsmobile stylists carried the taillights down into the rear bumper, creating a balanced look.

New Generation, New Goodies

General Motors introduced a more curvaceous body in the A-Body line for 1968, and the Oldsmobile Cutlass wore the slippery body well. Performance enthusiasts who wanted a small-block engine gravitated to the potent Ram Rod 350-ci-option W-31.

By the mid-1960s, General Motors saw that the A-platform underpinning most of its muscle cars was being dialed in for maximum performance but the body styling was getting a bit dated. For model year 1968, Oldsmobile, along with most of its GM cousins, unveiled curvaceous, head-turning vehicles on the trusty 112-inch-wheelbase A-platform.

Four-door sedans rode on a 116-inch wheelbase. Unlike prior years, the new-for-1968 body embraced the long hood/short deck proportions popularized by the Ford Mustang and embraced by youth buyers. Also, the 4-4-2 became a standalone model—no longer was it an option package on the Cutlass.

1968: 4-4-2 Bodystyles

For 1968, the 4-4-2 was available in three flavors: Holiday Coupe (hardtop), Sports Coupe (post), and as a convertible. Any way you ordered it, the 4-4-2 stood out from its more mainstream stablemates. Fore and aft, prominent 4-4-2 badging signaled that the top-range Oldsmobile performance car was on the prowl. Behind the front wheels, more 4-4-2 badging was fitted, highlighted by an optional vertical stripe that ran from the rocker panel to the top of the fender. Vent windows were installed in the doors; 1968 was the last year for that feature in the Holiday Coupe and the convertible, and the vent windows remained on the Sports Coupe through 1972.

Earlier 4-4-2s were broad-shouldered, beefy beasts. When the 1968 models were unveiled, the flowing lines and sloping rear window and trunk lid gave the new body a graceful look. Riding on 14-inch wheels, the vehicle tipped the scales at 3,713 pounds. Ride quality was impressive, as was handling prowess. Oldsmobile engineers crafted a suspension setup that resulted in the 4-4-2 becoming one of the best, if not the best, handling super cars of the day.

Anti-roll bars were fitted at each end: the front one was 0.937 inch in diameter, while the rear bar was 0.875 inch. Spring rates were handling-friendly: the front coils were 435 in-lbs, while the rears were 122 in-lbs. Reviewers of the day were unstinting in their praise of the 4-4-2's handling ability, saying that it allowed the driver to easily control the vehicle up to the limit, yet that it delivered a ride that was firm but didn't punish.

Power Options

General Motors continued to limit engine displacement for its intermediate vehicles to 400 ci (with the exception of the Corvette). Oldsmobile lived under the edict yet introduced a variety of 4-4-2 powerplants that covered a wide swath of tastes and budgets.

While a single displacement (400 ci) was offered, there were significant differences in the approach that Oldsmobile took to generate horsepower within a single-architecture engine. With a bore of 3.87 inches and a stroke of 4.25 inches, this was not a high-revving powerplant. Maximum torque of 440 ft-lbs came on at just 3,200 rpm.

400-ci W-30

The top-range 4-4-2 engine was fitted with W-30 forced-air induction and was rated at 360 hp at 5,400 rpm. The engine breathed through a revised set of 455-ci heads and used an Oldsmobile-only camshaft (part number 397328). As in earlier years, cool induction air was funneled into the air cleaner and single Rochester Quadrajet using a pair of flexible tubes attached to a pair of 13x2-inch scoops mounted beneath the front bumper outboard.

MotorTrend magazine tested a W-30-equipped 4-4-2 for its December 1967 issue. Using a Turbo Hydra-matic-equipped car, the quarter-mile took 15.3 seconds.

Oldsmobile priced the W-30 package at $263 for the 1968 4-4-2. This sum put an impressive slate of factory performance enhancements in the car, giving it 360 hp, which was 35 hp more than a standard 4-4-2. A pair of flexible tubes fed ambient air into the air-cleaner housing in an effort to extract a few more ponies from the 400-ci V-8.

The Cutlass S was a superb blend of performance, comfort, and quality. Add the W-31 option, and it took the performance part of the equation to a new level. Buyers' transmission choices were limited to manuals.

400-ci 350 hp

The next rung down on the 4-4-2 performance ladder was the 350-hp version. This was the standard engine for the 4-4-2 and the one that most buyers gravitated toward. It had a full range of transmissions available, starting with a 3-speed column shift. Next up were a pair of optional floor-mounted 4-speeds: a close-ratio (2.20:1 low gear), a wide-ratio (2.52:1), and lastly, the beefy Turbo Hydra-matic 3-speed automatic.

Shifting the automatic could be handled either on the column or by a floor-mounted shifter. The lead-foots at *Car Life* magazine spent a day wringing out this version equipped with the Turbo Hydra-matic transmission and 3.42:1 rear-axle ratio. The car came away with

a very respectable time of 15.13 seconds down the drag strip, tripping the lights at 92.2 mph. The *Car Life* reviewers were impressed with the price of the car too: $4,059 delivered. The buying public was impressed as well, and 36,641 units were sold for model year 1968.

400-ci 290 hp

The third 400-ci engine offering for 1968 was the Turnpike Cruiser option, which was a carryover from 1967. It used a 2-barrel carburetor, a Turbo Hydra-matic transmission with a 14.6:1 low gear, and a standard rear-axle ratio of 2.56:1. A pair of optional rear ratios, 2.78 and 3.08:1, ensured that the fuel tank drained at a slower

Oldsmobile's model-year 1968 performance offerings were an attractive blend of comfort and menace. The foreground model in the perfect period dress doesn't look quite ready for a campfire, but she got there in style. (Photo Courtesy General Motors)

rate than its more powerful versions. Rated at 290 hp, the Turnpike Cruiser boasted a healthy 425 ft-lbs of torque at just 2,400 rpm, which was more than enough to threaten the life expectancy of the rear tires.

W-31: Ram Rod 350

Not every path of Oldsmobile performance was paved with cubic inches. The crew at Oldsmobile Engineering created a small-block offering that injected no small amount of fun into the A-Body: the W-31 option. New for 1968, it was offered on regular Oldsmobile A-Body vehicles: the F-85 Club Coupe, the Cutlass standard coupe, and the Cutlass Supreme. Under the hood was the gold-painted 350-ci V-8—the Ram Rod 350. This was a no-nonsense setup that showed Oldsmobile was working hard to dispel its stodgy reputation.

Those who checked the order box for W-31 ended up with a powerplant that lived to rev. The heads (part number 5) were standard 350 parts, but Oldsmobile squeezed in the valves from its 455-ci engine: 2.00 intake/1.625-inch exhaust. The camshaft was aggressive (308-degree duration with 0.474-inch lift) to the point that its lopey idle didn't generate enough vacuum to allow for the fitment of power brakes.

Combined with 10.5:1 compression and a single massaged Rochester Quadrajet 750-cfm carburetor, the Ram Rod 350 pumped out 325 hp at 5,400 rpm and 390 ft-lbs of torque.

Unlike the 1967 W-30's intake ducting, which required the battery be mounted in the trunk, the 1968 W-31's air scoops were beneath the front bumper. This allowed the engineers to run the flexible tubing underneath the battery mounted in its normal position. W-31s used a larger harmonic balancer than a normal 350-ci engine. This engine was rated at 325 hp and 390 ft-lbs of torque, which was more than enough to leave souvenir lines on the road. It needed premium fuel to keep the 10.5:1-compression engine happy. A pair of brackets held the induction flexible tubing against the inner wheel well and away from the exhaust manifolds. Oldsmobile only built 742 Ram Rod 350s in 1968.

For 1968, Oldsmobile mounted the W-31's induction scoops beneath the ends of the front bumper. The W-31 came equipped with both front and rear anti-sway bars. The orange tag visible under the front of the vehicle is attached to the front bar.

Lithe, curvaceous, and a fresh design, the General Motors A-Body redesign hit showrooms for the 1968 model year. The perimeter frames wheelbase was shortened from 115-inches to 112, and used a short/long arm (SLA) front suspension, and a four-link rear setup. The W-31's beefy 350-ci engine was an ideal powerplant for melting rear tires while maintaining impressive handling.

From the rear, it was impossible to determine if this 1968 Cutlass S was equipped with the potent Ram Rod 350, unless you could hear the exhaust note. The flowing lines debuted on the 1968 models.

The cylinders were honed to *D* specs, and *A* pistons with a larger skirt clearance were used. Transmission choices were straight-forward: either a 3-speed or 4-speed manual. Induction airflow was cribbed from the W-30, meaning that the flex tubes ran from the under-bumper scoops to the air cleaner. Black plastic front fender liners (slightly) lightened the weight on the front tires.

On the drag strip, the W-31 jumped to 60 mph in 14.9 seconds and crossed the line at 96 mph. Oldsmobile built just 674 W-31s for 1968 and 38 W-31 factory drag cars. These numbers were encouraging to the decision makers at Oldsmobile, and they pushed to make 1969 at least as successful as 1968 was. They wouldn't be disappointed.

The very picture of discretion, the 1968 W-31 was fitted with these decals next to the front side-marker lights to announce the presence of the straight-line missile. The W-31's aggressive camshaft gave the engine a lope at idle that suggested that things were going to get very busy very quickly.

The W-31 package was available on a wide range of Oldsmobile A-Bodies in 1968, including the Cutlass S. This well-equipped example was fitted with the optional shoulder belts. Every W-31 in 1968 had three pedals.

Oldsmobile used the Rocket nomenclature to denote performance engines from 1949 on, and for the 1968 model year, the W-31 fully embraced the concept. The small-block V-8 was essentially an engine intended for drag strip use and stuffed into a street-legal car. The camshaft was so radical that it didn't generate enough vacuum at idle to supply power brakes, so that option wasn't offered in W-31s.

Oldsmobile stylists retained the horizontal quad headlight motif in the 1969 Cutlass line, including the W-31. It's evident here that driving the Ram Rod 350 in snow could be a problem with the low-hanging scoops. Officially, the W-31 name was not on the car in 1968, but that changed in 1969.

Only a manual transmission was available in the 1968 Ram Rod 350. Choices were the M20 wide-ratio gearbox, the M21 close-ratio transmission, and the M14 3-speed manual. While the transmissions were built by Muncie, the shifter was pure Hurst.

The Super Stock II stamped-steel wheel (option code N66) on the 1968 Ram Rod 350 was handsome, tough, and measured 14 x 6 inches.

Because the Ram Rod 350 was available in a wide range of Cutlass models, it was possible to get one with a front bench seat. Note that the steering wheel is color matched to the interior. This was the base wheel.

Hurst/Olds

Famed racer Jack "Doc" Watson, George Hurst's go-to guy, met with Oldsmobile Chief Engineer John B. Beltz in 1965, and the two hit it off straightaway. Watson felt that Oldsmobile had the best engineering department, yet the division's performance was losing sales every year. Traditional customers were dying off, and unless the division could change its public perception, the slide downward would continue. So, Watson proposed to Beltz that Oldsmobile should consider building a Super 4-4-2 as a way of garnering attention from a younger market.

In the excellent book *Setting the Pace: Oldsmobile's First 100 Years* by Helen Jones Earley and James R. Walkinshaw, Watson recounted how the Hurst/Olds concept was born, as well how Oldsmobile performance options came to have *W* prefixes.

"The H/O was born in a meeting with Beltz and Bob Dorshimer," as stated in the book. "We had been working on performance options and various other things. There wasn't really a budget for high-performance options, so we kept putting [them] under the Pure Oil trials and Mobil gas economy runs . . . [Beltz was] a maverick. He wanted to do things, yet he was a corporate player and knew where the boundaries were. [So, he also] knew I was the only shot he had to get past the boundaries. That's how the Hurst/Oldsmobile was conceived."

During that meeting, Watson said, "Beltz says to Dorshimer . . . 'What prefixes have we got left for options? Have we still got the Js?' 'No, we're using the Js for something else.' [Beltz says,] 'Doc's always beating us up about wanting to have a J-4 and J-7 and all these other things. How about Ws?' [Dorshimer says,] 'Yeah, Ws open.' [Beltz said,] 'Good. We'll [label] these performance options

HAIR GROWING POTION FOR A 4-4-2

Hair Growing Ingredients:

- Two 1966 425 cubic inch Oldsmobile engines, specially outfitted with fuel injection units and modified 6:71 GMC superchargers.

- Two Toronado transmissions and drive trains to supply more than 1,000 horsepower to both front and rear wheels.

- Mount these brutish assemblies in a specially constructed tubular frame and roll bar designed by Hurst Performance Research Center.

- Install special hood, trunk lid, bumpers and other body components formed from weight-saving aluminum.

- Equip with dual spot disc brakes and add a pair of Simpson Drag Chutes mounted in the tail light assemblies for added safety.

Directions For Mixing and Serving:

- Mix above items thoroughly and pour into a well-gutted, lightweight 4-4-2 Oldsmobile. Turn on both throttles for nine seconds and you will have clouds of horsepower produced smoke for a quarter-mile.

"Gentleman" Joe Schubeck piloted the Hurst Hairy Olds, which featured two 425-ci engines with more than 1,000 hp on each one.

[with] Ws, so every time I'm in trouble for being over budget . . . I'll remember Watson did it to me.'"

The first result of this collaboration was the 1966 W-30 package, and by 1969, the time was at hand to see about busting through GM's limit of 400 ci for intermediates. As far as the suits at General Motors were aware, engine-less 4-4-2s were being shipped to Demmer Engineering in Lansing, Michigan, where 455-ci engines were being installed, making the Hurst/Olds an aftermarket conversion. In actuality, the huge engines were installed at the Oldsmobile factory before being shipped to Demmer. But the entire project almost didn't come to fruition. Watson recalled the following in *Setting the Pace*.

"So, Tuesday morning, we got all these players together. It was a very candid meeting. There was no screaming, shouting, whatever; it was just everybody voicing their concerns. John [Beltz] says to Mac Worden, 'How about if we sent out a red release on the thing?' Back then, when a red release hits the zones, it didn't matter what was going on, you dropped what you were doing and did what was on that release. [Worden] said yes. 'And if we don't have at least 150 orders by Friday, we won't do

It was an everyday occurrence in 1969 to open an automotive enthusiast magazine and see an advertisement for tire-shredding performance wrapped in a flashy body. Targeting the extrovert in the crowd, this 1969 Hurst/Olds ad spelled out what it took to create an instant legend.

the project. Is that fair enough, Doc?' I said, 'Sure.' Well, by Thursday afternoon, we had [close to 1,700 orders]. It was nuts. [But] it was fun to go to that meeting on Friday. I mean, these poor guys are [thinking] 'How could we be so wrong?' . . . So needless to say, everybody jumped behind it, and away we went."

The 1968 result was impressive. Finished in Peruvian Silver and Black, a massive 455-ci engine rated at 390 hp at 5,500 rpm and a brutal 500 ft-lbs of torque at 3,600 rpm was fitted. Ironically, the 455 engine was

OLDSMOBILE AND THE QUARTER-MILE

We've seen how Oldsmobile dominated NASCAR in the early days of the series, but that wasn't the only form of motorsports in which the automaker successfully competed. Quarter-mile drag strips grew in popularity in the late 1950s, blossoming in popularity throughout the 1960s and beyond. Oldsmobile powerplants had long proven their durability and ability to generate serious grunt, which were valuable attributes in the world of drag racing.

One of the more successful builder/racers of the sport's early days was Jack Kulp, from Langhorne, Pennsylvania. He favored Rocket 88 engines in the early 1950s and was more than a drag strip racer. In February 1956, he piloted his 1954 Oldsmobile Rocket 88 coupe to 130.909 mph on the sands of Daytona Beach, Florida.

With the creation of the NHRA, drag racing for the most part left the public roads and became a mainstream sport at proper drag strips. One of the early successes was the LA-based Albertson Olds team with an Oldsmobile-powered dragster. It was owned by Ronnie Scrima and Gene Adams and was driven by Leonard Harris. The supercharged engine sat in a modified Chassis Research K-88, and in the 1960 summer racing season, it was the car to beat. Its 462-ci powerplant helped it win 12 consecutive Saturday-night races at Lions Drag Strip in Long Beach, California. At the 1960 NHRA U.S. National in Detroit, Michigan, the Oldsmobile bested a field of 36 entries to take the Top Eliminator crown.

In September 1960, the Albertson Olds, with Harris behind the wheel, covered the quarter-mile in 8.96 seconds at 171.42 mph. Unfortunately, Harris was killed in October during a race in another car. Driving duties in the Albertson Olds were picked up by Tom McEwen, who went on to have a long career in the sport.

Another head-turner was the *Hurst Hairy Olds*, which was developed by Hurst, John Beltz, and Doc Watson and campaigned during the 1966 season. With a pair of 425-ci supercharged V-8s bolted to a pair of Toronado transaxles, this crowd pleaser would smoke all four tires the length of the drag strip. It was designed to showcase the durability of the new chain-driven automatic transmission in the Toronado. Another dual-engine all-wheel-drive Toronado was the guardrail jumping *Terrifying Toronado*, campaigned by John Smyser.

The 1966 4-4-2 was built on GM's intermediate platform, which was used by Buick to build the Skylark and by Chevrolet to build the Chevelle. Oldsmobile had success with the bodystyle, which is shown here in the F-85 Club Coupe 4-4-2 W-30 configuration. The division used very subtle badging on the car, letting its performance do the talking.

With the racing ban in force at General Motors during the early days of the 4-4-2, ways had to be found to get Oldsmobile performance on the drag strip without waving a red flag at the GM executive floor. John Beltz and engineer Dale Smith backed the efforts of Brainbeau Olds in Braintree, Massachusetts. Considerable success on the quarter-mile ensued, although some of the suits at General Motors had reservations.

Hemmings magazine recounted Dale Smith receiving a phone call "from a GM executive who warned him that he could be in trouble for violating GM's racing ban." Smith told the executive he was "not afraid of getting into trouble unless a pinhead like him would squeal to the head of General Motors. I told him 'The bottom line on why you, I, or anyone else is here is to sell cars. I'm trying to improve Olds's youth image and cultivate new customers. If you can't understand that concept, you might as well piss in your whiskey.'"

Brainbeau Olds's 4-4-2 was a stormer, garnering many wins, including the 1966 NHRA U.S. Nationals driven by Loyed Woodward. When Brainbeau Olds went under, Berejik Oldsmobile of Needham, Massachusetts, picked up where Brainbeau left off. It didn't take long for Berejik to see results from backing a race team.

Dick Smothers, of the Smothers Brothers comedy duo, was an active fan of drag racing in the late 1960s and early 1970s. His team ran Oldsmobiles in the Stock classes, and Dick Smothers's personal race car was prepped by Doc Watson. The team that the brothers assembled was well funded and placed well until the Smothers brothers stepped away from racing at the close of the 1971 season.

George Berejik recalled: "Monday morning the phone would be ringing right away: 'Do you have a red 4-4-2?' 'Do you have a green 4-4-2?' 'Bench seat?' 'Bucket seat?' It really boosted our business, all our business. It was really profitable. It compounded into many other sales. Other Oldsmobile dealers that did not race fed off our success on the track." Berejik ended up working with the comedy duo the Smothers Brothers as they campaigned an Oldsmobile on the drag strip. That effort lasted three years.

Oldsmobile's involvement with drag racing came about due to the rivalry with Chevrolet. Traditionally, Chevrolet had been the performance division, and the success of Oldsmobile on the drag strip ruffled feathers at Chevrolet so much so that the vice president at Chevy lobbied the president of General Motors in 1971 to make the Bowtie division the only motorsports division. That spelled the end of factory backing.

evolution of a winner...

The ultimate expression of the American "Supercar" is now available in Oldsmobile showrooms across the country.

This one-of-a-kind vehicle is a limited quantity reproduction of a unique 4-4-2 concept designed as a personal car for George Hurst, president of Hurst-Campbell, Inc.

The design was conceived for Hurst by Jack (Doc) Watson, well known to automotive enthusiasts as an innovator of special event vehicles and for his many contributions to the advancement of motor sports throughout the United States.

As soon as Watson had completed the car for Hurst and it had been shown to several Oldsmobile dealers, a high degree of enthusiasm generated requests for additional copies.

One such request came from an industrialist friend of Watson's in Lansing, Michigan, by the name of John Demmer. Long an auto enthusiast, Demmer also has a son who strongly influences his interests, and he asked for two cars—one for his own collection and another for his son.

Watson informed Demmer of the 'word-of-mouth' interest and subsequent requests, especially the enthusiastic response shown by several Oldsmobile dealers, whereupon Demmer offered to set up and custom build a limited quantity of Hurst-Oldsmobiles.

A meeting was scheduled to introduce Demmer to George Hurst, and the project was under way. Immediately, Hurst and Watson met with Oldsmobile Division management and their reaction was highly favorable.

After a series of exhaustive tests and thorough component evaluation, the vehicle is now ready for production with Hurst modifications done by Demmer Engineering in Lansing.

Powered by a custom built 455 cubic inch engine, the Hurst-Olds will be available in both pillar coupe and hardtop coupe versions. Special features of the Hurst-Olds (also called the H-O) include the following items:

- "One-of-a-kind" competition silver and black paint scheme
- 455 cu. in. high-performance engine □ 390 horsepower at 5000 R.P.M. □ 500 ft. lb. of torque at 3600 R.P.M. □ High performance cylinder heads □ High lift, long duration camshaft □ Special machined crankshaft, distributor curve and carburetor jetting
- Modified Turbo Hydra-Matic transmission, insuring complete manual control
- Force-Air induction system
- Hurst dual-gate shifter and console—the most versatile automatic transmission control for the enthusiast
- Oversize G70 x 14 Goodyear poly-glass tires. (These tires, revolutionary in their design, put more horsepower to the ground, and insure outstanding handling and braking.)
- Distinctive Hurst-Olds exterior emblems
- Specially trimmed instrument panel & interior emblem
- Highly efficient front wheel disc brakes as standard equipment with a sensitive front to rear proportioning valve to insure accurate braking action
- Heavy-duty rear end assembly—including extra strength gears and axle shafts
- Heavy-duty 4-4-2 suspension and rear stabilizer (a suspension system highly acclaimed by most enthusiast magazine editors)
- High capacity cooling—special calibrated viscous fan clutch, thicker—higher density radiator core insures cooling, even under the hardest use.

The above package is designed to give the enthusiast uncompromising street performance that will exceed any vehicle of its type, not only in outstanding acceleration but also in handling, riding and braking characteristics.

The Hurst-Olds has all the muscle characteristics of the finest super car, but without objectionable interior noise and choppy ride.

Oldsmobile's original factory warranty will not be altered as all modification components are approved and released by Oldsmobile product engineering with the exception of the Hurst dual-gate shifter and console, which are protected by an unconditional lifetime guarantee from Hurst-Campbell, Inc.

Seeing is believing... owning is unreal

Remember when . . . in 1949 "Stage I" of the Olds Rocket "blasted off" and revolutionized the auto industry!

Get ready for "Stage II" . . .

The H/O's special one-of-a-kind paint scheme, coupled with special exterior emblems immediately sets you apart from the "pack" . . . and brands you a leader!

Oldsmobile touted its heritage by referencing the 1949 Rocket engine (Stage 1), which some have argued laid the groundwork for what would become the muscle car. Oldsmobile took its 1968 Hurst/Olds one step further, noting that these 455-equipped super cars were the beginning of Stage 2. (Photo Courtesy General Motors)

12 pounds lighter than the 400-ci powerplant. The transmission choice was simple: the 3-speed Turbo Hydra-matic automatic. A manual transmission was not available with the Hurst/Olds. Suspension upgrades created a secure, highly competent handling machine that was able to surprise many who thought the Hurst/Olds was only built for a straight line.

In a straight line, the 1968 Hurst/Olds was no slouch. Fitted with the W-30's forced-air induction system, it could knock back the quarter-mile in 14 seconds at 99 mph. Two different W designators were used for the engine. If the Hurst/Olds was built without air-conditioning, the engine was a W45. If air-conditioning was installed, it was called a W46.

More than 3,000 orders were received, but the capacity at Demmer limited the number of vehicles built. When 1968's Hurst/Olds line was wrapped, 515 units had been built (451 Holiday Coupes and 64 Sport Coupes). Additionally, there were four convertibles converted by Hurst Performance for promotional use. The first 1968 Hurst/Olds was shipped on May 24, 1958, and the last Hurst/Olds was shipped on July 12, 1968. Hurst advertising of the day boasted, "Seeing is believing . . . Owning is unreal." They can't be accused of exaggeration.

For 1969, Oldsmobile followed its first act with 906 Hurst/Olds. In total, 16,537 H/Os were created, making the third-party parts supplier and auto manufacturer easily the most successful cross-promotion muscle car of the whole era.

Hurst/Olds Production Numbers	
Year	**Production**
1968	515
1969	906
1972	633
1973	1,097
1974	1,851
1975	2,535
1979	2,499
1983	3,001
1984	3,500
Total	**16,537**

It could be argued that Oldsmobile's most aggressive styling cues came to fruition upon the 1969 Hurst Olds. Conceived by show car builder Styline Customs, nearly every aspect of its design made the production model.

From the back, a Hurst/Olds is immediately identifiable with its spoiler and wide gold stripe traversing the center of the car. An H/O emblem also sat affixed to the lower right hand of the decklid.

A 455-ci engine was forced into the Hurst/Olds engine bay. GM had its displacement ban, but because a third party was doing the build (Hurst), Oldsmobile had their go-around in place.

Air-gobbling snorkels forced a strong breeze into the awaiting air cleaner below. The engine displacement adorned each side of the snorkel.

The 1969 Hurst/Olds left nothing off the table when it came to performance. Other than GM's COPO program, this was one of the other very few methods of acquiring more than 400 ci under the hood of an intermediate A-Body. (Photo Courtesy General Motors)

1969 HURST/OLDS SPECIFICATIONS

GENERAL

Model	Modified 4-4-2 Holiday Coupe
Wheelbase	112.0
Length, overall	201.9
Width, overall	76.2
Height, overall	52.8
Track, front	61.0
Track, rear	60.0
Weight	3716 lbs.

ENGINE

Type	90° OHV V-8
Bore and Stroke	4.125 x 4.250
Displacement, cubic inches	455
Compression Ratio	10.5:1
Horsepower (@ rpm)	380 @ 5000
Torque (lb./ft. @ rpm)	500 @ 3200
Carburetor	4-bbl. Rochester 4 MV

ENGINE (Cont.)

Fuel	Premium
Air Induction	Special Cold Air w/ Hood Scoop
Intake Valve Duration	285°
Exhaust Valve Duration	287°
Valve Opening Overlap	57°
Valve Lift	0.472
Valve Lifters	Hydraulic
Exhaust System	Dual

TRANSMISSION (Std.)

Name	Turbo Hydra-Matic
Type	Modified 3-Speed Torque Converter
Gear Ratio, low	2.48
Gear Ratio, second	1.48
Gear Ratio, third	1.00
Gear Ratio, reverse	2.08
Torque Converter Ratio	2.30
Shift Mechanism	Hurst Dual/Gate

REAR AXLE

Type	Salisbury Live Hypoid, Semi Floating
Differential	Limited Slip, Multiple Plate Clutch
Axle Ratio (Std.)	3.42
Axle Ratio (Opt.)	3.91
Axle Ratio (A/C)	3.23

TIRES

Type and Manufacturer	Bias-Belted Goodyear Polyglas®
Size	F60 x 15

WHEELS

Type	Welded Steel
Size and Flange	15 x 7 JJ

BRAKES

Type	Power
Front	11 inch Disc
Rear	9.5 inch Drum

All dimensions are in inches unless otherwise indicated.

While the information herein was in effect when approved for printing, Hurst Performance Research Inc. reserves the right to change specifications, design or prices without notice and without liability therefor.

HURST PERFORMANCE RESEARCH INC.

10711 NORTHEND, FERNDALE, MICHIGAN 48220

ADVERTISING OLDSMOBILE PERFORMANCE

Oldsmobile was late to the performance car party. Sure, it had its able Rocket engines in the 1950s, but the real battle for street supremacy began with the 1964 Pontiac GTO. It didn't take long for the rest of the domestic auto manufacturers to step up and release competitive vehicles. In the fight for customers, each carmaker used different advertising agencies to craft campaigns to woo the young and young at heart into the showroom.

Chicago-based advertising agency Leo Burnett Co. acquired the Oldsmobile account in 1967 when Burnett bought the D. P. Brother Co. agency. Brother had handled the Oldsmobile account since 1934. Oldsmobile wasn't sure about the muscle car landscape when the 4-4-2 debuted, and advertisements from that era are quaint, showing the muscle car sometimes as a photo, sometimes an illustration, against hand drawings.

As its competitors raised their advertising games, Oldsmobile followed suit, creating one of the most memorable ad campaigns in auto history: Dr. Oldsmobile. Along with his henchmen, the good doctor was busy assembling Frankenstein-like automotive creations that took on a life of their own. Borrowing heavily from classic horror films, these were high-dollar ads with extravagant settings, lighting, and props. Dealerships could even outfit a corner of their showrooms to replicate a Dr. Oldsmobile ad using signage and material from Oldsmobile.

With the collapse of the performance car market, Oldsmobile concentrated on mainstream buyers using a more mainstream approach to advertising. Like its competitors in the 1970s, Oldsmobile's ads showed the vehicle in an ideal lifestyle setting with a stunningly lit car surrounded by people enjoying the good life, which was attainable because they chose Oldsmobile. Famed

Performance was starting to return to Oldsmobile in 1985, and what better way to let people know than to resurrect the 4-4-2 name. As in days of yore, the all-around package was advertised: healthy power under the hood, a performance-savvy suspension, and full instrumentation. The two-tone paint on the limited-edition model was handsome and head-turning. (Photo Courtesy General Motors)

Olds Cutlass 442.
The legend returns.

There's a legend on the loose. Olds Cutlass 442 is back. Production is strictly limited. But the lucky few who manage to snare one will share a vivid—repeat, vivid—recollection of what the good old days were all about.

The equipment? A high output 5-liter V-8 feeds low restriction dual outlet exhausts. And to help you keep tabs on all that horsepower, the cockpit comes equipped with full instrumentation.

A specially tuned suspension dusts off hairpin turns, courtesy of Pliacel-lined front and load leveler rear shocks, stiff front and rear stabilizer bars and Goodyear Eagle GT's on super stock wheels.

Sure, this is heavy-duty gear. And when it's put together in an Olds, you get more than good hardware. You get the stuff legends are made of.

Oldsmobiles are equipped with engines produced at facilities operated by GM car groups, subsidiaries or affiliated companies worldwide.

442 Oldsmobile

Let's get it together...buckle up.

There is a special feel in an *Oldsmobile*

By the time this advertisement for the 1990 Cutlass Calais Quad 442 hit magazine shelves, General Motors was moving to pull the plug on its oldest division. Sales had been trending downward, and the corporation was looking to cut costs. After the disastrous Not Your Father's Oldsmobile campaign, some in the company thought that putting the historic 442 name on a vehicle would create nostalgic sales. That didn't happen. (Photo Courtesy General Motors)

Detroit automotive studio Boulevard Photographic created many of these iconic images. The copy was rich with comfort details that outlined how superior the vehicle, and by extension the buyer, was in making the choice to purchase an Oldsmobile

As the 1980s rolled into the 1990s, General Motors decided that Buick should handle the customer base that embraced large, comfortable vehicles, while Oldsmobile was tasked with going after import buyers. In 1988, the slogan written by creative director Joel Machak, "Not Your Father's Oldsmobile," debuted as part of a song written by Don Gwaltney and was paired with the tag line "The New Generation of Olds." This was seen by many as stepping away from the division's traditional buyers and chasing younger customers.

A bevy of entertainment personalities were enlisted to appear in various ads, including ex-Beatle Ringo Starr, Albert Einstein's great-grandson Edward, and actors Peter Graves and William Shatner, which was not exactly a younger demographic. The campaign didn't go as planned. How harsh was the reaction? For model year 1986, Oldsmobile sold 1,050,832 vehicles. Model year 1990 saw just 489,492 units. The campaign was a bust.

Many Oldsmobile dealers were not pleased with the softening sales in the early 1990s and blamed the lackluster ad campaign of the day. General Manager John Rock called for a review of the agency's annual $140 million account in 1993, and after a grueling five-month review process, Leo Burnett USA kept the account.

However, sales continued to inch downward as fresh buyers failed to materialize, which was a shame because Oldsmobile had a very good product line. The damage in public perception had been done. In 2000, sales were 237,399, which was a fraction of prior years. Oldsmobile was shut down in 2004. Marketing had failed Oldsmobile.

The Oldsmobile A-Body was not the only offering from the division to be involved with the W process. This 1969 Toronado was one of 2,844 built that year, and as a $47.39 option, it was one of the best performance deals in history. The W-34 package transformed the car into a Rocket.

W-34 Toronado: Bully in a Tuxedo

The muscle car war was heating up as the 1960s churned on, and Oldsmobile was in the fray with the 4-4-2 and W-30. Bigger was better, and the performance enthusiasts within Oldsmobile felt that there was a market for an over-the-top gentleman's express. The closest offering on the Oldsmobile menu was the revolutionary Toronado, a front-wheel-drive, two-door personal car. Equipped with the beefy 455-ci V-8 rated at 375 hp, it was a freeway cruiser of the first magnitude. However, there's always a hunger for more. More power usually. Enter RPO W-34.

Oldsmobile fit the W-34 with a hotter camshaft in the 455 engine, dual low-restriction exhaust, cold-air induction via ducting from the driver-side fender into

---

TORONADO
Models • Equipment • Prices
9487 Toronado

STANDARD EQUIPMENT

- Armrests with Ashtrays, Built-in Front and Rear
- Battery, 75-Amp.-Hr./90-Plate
- Brakes, Pedal-Ease Power
- Cigar Lighter, Instrument Panel
- Clock, Electric
- Delcotron, 42-Ampere
- Engine, 375-hp Rocket 455 V-8 H.C. (4-bbl. carburetor)
- Floor Carpeting, Wall-to-Wall (plus carpeted cowl, door and front seat-back lower panels)
- Lamps, Front Armrest Ashtray
- Lamps, Instrument Panel Courtesy and Glove Compartment
- Lamps, Roof Rear-Quarter
- Lamp Switches, Automatic Door
- Moldings, Chrome Rocker Panel and Wheel-Opening
- Moldings, Chrome Roof Drip
- Moldings, Chrome Side Window Sill
- Pedals, Chrome-Accented
- Seat, Bench Front
- Seat Cushions, Foam-Padded Front and Rear
- Seat Lap Belts, 3 Front and 3 Rear
- Seat Shoulder Belts, 2 Front
- Seat Moldings, Bright, Front (Seat Side and Backrest)
- Steering, Roto-Matic Power
- Steering Wheel, Deluxe
- Tires, 8.85 x 15" 2-Ply Blackwall

- Transmission, Turbo Hydra-Matic (column-shift)
- Wheel Hub Caps
- Windshield Wipers, Recessed-Park

FACTORY-INSTALLED OPTIONS

A01 Windows, Soft-Ray Tinted—Includes A02 .... $ 47.39

A02 Windshield, Soft-Ray Tinted .... $ 28.12

A31 Windows, Power Side $104.00

A42 Seat Adjuster, 6-Way Power—For bench seat .... $ 94.79

A46 Seat Adjuster, 4-Way Power—For left-hand bucket seat. A51 required .... $ 69.51

A69 Seat Backrest, Reclining Strato Bench—For right-hand side. Y69 required. A81 recommended .... $ 31.60

A70 Seat Backrest, Reclining Strato Bucket—For right-hand seat. A81 recommended. A51 or Y69 required .... $ 31.60

A81 Seat Head Restraints, Dual Front—For Strato Seats. A51 or Y69 required ... $ 52.66

A82 Seat Head Restraints, Dual Front—For standard bench seat. N.A. with Y69 . $ 42.13

AS5 Seat Shoulder Belts, Rear:
To match standard seat belts ...... $ 23.17
To match deluxe seat belts .... $ 26.33

A91 Trunk-Lid Latch, Power .... $ 13.69

A93 Door Locks Power .... $ 44.76

B32 Floor Mats, Auxiliary Front ...... $ 10.00

B33 Floor Mats, Auxiliary Rear .... $ 7.37

B36 Trunk Floor Mat, Heavy-Duty ...... $ 7.90

B93 Moldings, Chrome Door-Edge Guard $ 5.27

C08 Rooftop Covering, Vinyl—N.A. with Y70 .... $121.12

C50 Window Defogger, Rear .... $ 21.06

C60 Air Conditioner, Four-Season $421.28

C61 Air Conditioner, Comfortron $500.27

D33 Mirror, Remote-Control Outside Rearview .... $ 9.48

D55 Console, Sports—Includes shift mechanism, lockable map case with lamp, and front and rear console lamps .... $ 47.39

G66 Shock Absorbers, Superlift Rear .... $ 42.13

J52 Brakes, Power with Front Disc ..... $ 78.99

K30 Cruise Control, Automatic .... $ 78.99

K66 Engine Ignition System, Ultra-High-Voltage $100.05

M55 Oil Cooler, Automatic Transmission Auxiliary —For trailer towing .... $ 15.80

N37 Steering Wheel, Tilt-and-Telescope—Includes special steering wheel ...... $ 78.99

N98 Wheels and Trim Rings, Chrome Open-Spider .... $ 89.52

P03 Wheel Discs, Deluxe .... $ 40.02

P04 Tires, 8.85 x 15" 2-Ply Whitewall ....$ 48.76

P06 Wheel Trim Rings, Chrome .... $ 18.43

T87 Lamps, Cornering .... $ 36.86

U57 Stereo Tape Player—Includes rear speaker. U58, U59 or U63 required:
Without U58 .... $133.76
With U58 .... $116.91

U58 Radio, AM-FM Stereophonic—Includes rear speaker $238.03

U59 Radio, AM-FM Signal-Seeker Tuning $173.78

U63 Radio, Deluxe Pushbutton .... $ 86.89

U71 Radio Antenna, Power (Front) ..... $ 29.12

U80 Radio Speaker, Bi-Phonic Rear .... $ 16.85

U89 Wiring Harness, Trailer Electrical .. $ 10.63

W34 Engine Induction System, Force-Air—Includes 400-hp Rocket 455 V-8, dual exhaust outlets and high-performance camshaft $210.64

W39 Seat Belts, Deluxe Front and Rear Lap and Front Shoulder:
With Bucket Seats .... $ 11.06
Without Bucket Seats .... $ 12.64

Y60 Lamps and Mirror, Convenience—Includes trunk and underhood lamps, visor vanity mirror. Includes door courtesy and open-door warning lamps with Y69:
With Y69 .... $ 19.69
Without Y69 .... $ 6.53

Y69 Interior, Custom—Includes Strato Bench or Strato Bucket Front Seats; custom upholstery, sidewall trim panels, door pull handles, cigar lighters in ashtrays $173.78

Y70 Paint, G. T. Stripe—N.A. with C08 ... $ 10.53

Y72 Engine-Cooling Equipment, Heavy-Duty—Includes special radiator, heavy-duty water pump, Thermo-Cool engine fan and 55-ampere Delcotron:
With C60 or C61 .... $ 5.27
Without C60 or C61 .... $ 57.93

FACTORY-INSTALLED ACCESSORY GROUPS

CODE	ACCESSORY		GROUP 1	
A91	Trunk-Lid Latch, Power	X	X	X
B93	Moldings, Chrome Door-Edge Guard	X	X	X
U58	Radio, AM-FM Stereophonic			X
U59	Radio, AM-FM Signal-Seeker Tuning		X	
U63	Radio, Deluxe Pushbutton	X		
Y60	Lamps and Mirror, Convenience	X	X	X
	Price*	With Y69	$125.54	$212.43	$276.68
		Without Y69	$112.38	$199.27	$263.52

*Group price is the sum of the prices of all accessories within the group. Desired option of radio must be specified.

Way over on the left-hand column in the 1968 Oldsmobile brochure was code W-34 for the Engine Induction System on the 1968 Toronado. For $210.64, you got the 455 Rocket, dual exhaust, and a high-performance camshaft. (Photo Courtesy General Motors)

Under the huge hood was a potent 455-ci V-8 bolted to a modified Turbo Hydra-matic transmission and a heavy-duty torque converter. The front-wheel-drive personal car was loaded with options, and the big engine had no problem supplying power for everything. The W-34 powerplant was rated at 400 hp and a massive 500 ft-lbs of torque.

Only Toronado W-34s wore this OM tag, denoting a Turbo Hydra-matic modified for heavy duty. With the huge engine and transmission over the front wheels, traction from the front-wheel-drive system wasn't an issue.

the air cleaner housing (1968 only), and heat-treated valve springs. The 3-speed automatic transmission was the Turbo Hydra-matic 425, a modified TH350 fitted with a higher-stall-speed torque converter.

The engine was a low-revving affair with substantial 10.25:1 compression. Peak horsepower was listed at 400 at 4,800 rpm. Torque was not in short supply, as 500 ft-lbs came to a peak at just 3,200 rpm. The final drive axle ratio was 3.07:1, keeping engine RPM low at highway speeds. Road tests of the era noted that the big car would move from 0-60 mph in 7.5 seconds on its way to a top speed of 135 mph. The car visited the drag strip at the hands of *Car and Driver* (January 1970) and performed well: 15.7 seconds at 89.8 mph. That's pretty good for a vehicle knocking on 4,400 pounds.

The W-34 option, when introduced in 1968, cost $210.64, and Oldsmobile sold only 124 units. For 1969 and 1970, the division lowered the price to $47.39, and sales took a noticeable jump. Oldsmobile moved 2,844 cars in 1969, and as word got around about the potent nature of the option, 5,341 went to good homes in 1970.

The year 1969 saw the introduction of the Toronado GT W-34, a one-year offering. However, Oldsmobile saw the writing on the wall: high-performance vehicles would soon be extinct. So, the decision was made to cease production after the 1970 run. Today, W-34s are a collector's item—a very potent collector's item.

Being a front-wheel-drive vehicle, the 1969 Toronado W-34 had a flat floor in the interior, opening up leg room for middle occupants of the front seat. Look carefully through the steering wheel, and you can make out the rolling drum speedometer.

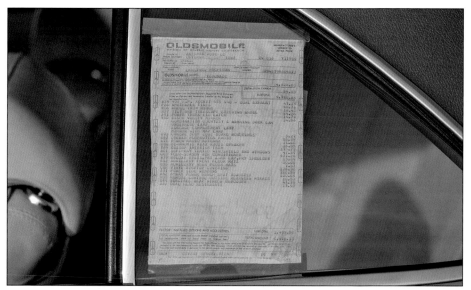

Being a luxury model Oldsmobile with performance enhancements, this gentleman's express didn't come cheap. The price as delivered was $6,378.15. In 1969, that was a lot of money for a personal vehicle.

Toronado W-34s had a sensor in the radiator that automatically opened the headlight doors if the coolant temperature got too high. The lights wouldn't come on, but the increased airflow would hold the engine temp within spec.

1969: Evolutionary Improvements

It didn't take a rocket scientist to see that the performance car battle in America was heating up. By 1969, virtually every domestic carmaker had entries in the super car club—even little American Motors Corporation (AMC). Ironically, AMC introduced a vehicle in 1957 that was years ahead of the classic muscle car formula: the Rambler Rebel. Fitted with a 327-ci engine in an intermediate body (sound familiar?), it could even be equipped with factory Bendix Electrojector electronic fuel injection.

The trend started by the 1964 Pontiac GTO had blossomed into a tidal wave of performance cars working to outdo the competition. Oldsmobile, which was long regarded as an old man's car, had entered the

1960s behind the performance curve. However, by 1969, the division had transformed itself into a source of top-shelf, tire-shredding explosive power that was cloaked in an attractive body with a comfortable interior. It was a gentleman's express, indeed.

Like every GM division, Oldsmobile knew that significant body changes were planned for the 1970 model year, so visually, the offerings for 1969 had only minor exterior changes, which was cost-effective for the division. Unlike years later when tape and decals were sometimes the only difference between model years, the 1969 Cutlass line received pronounced front and rear changes. From the center of the hood waterfalling into the center of the front bumper to the vertical taillights inset into the trunk lid and bumper, the changes were subtle but effective. Unknown to buyers in 1969, these changes foreshadowed the following years.

4-4-2

The 4-4-2 was alive and well, and the W-codes were going strong. All 1969 4-4-2s, and by extension Ws, were built at the Oldsmobile plant in Lansing, Michigan. As before, the engine displacement was limited to 400 ci, yet the Hurst/Olds 1969 edition retained the 455 engine.

Engine outputs in the 4-4-2 varied depending on the choice of transmission. Spring for a manual box, and the engine was rated at 350 hp. Check the automatic transmission, and the engine was 325 hp. Then, there was the W-30.

The W-30, a $264 option, was not changed from the year prior; eagle-eyed spotters looked for the distinctive under-bumper scoops. For the less observant, Oldsmobile designers laid on a pair of W-30 decals above the front side-marker lights. Under the long hood, the W-30's 400-ci engine still cranked out 360 hp, which was enough to power the car to a top speed of 123 mph. As in 1968, the W-30 engine used the beefy crankshaft and connecting rods from the 455 engine for durability.

New cast-iron exhaust manifolds were introduced using individual runners to improve flow. The internal runners started right at the exhaust port of the *D* heads. Red inner fender wells were still part of the package with hand-cut holes made in the lower portion to allow the flex tubing used in the induction system to reach the air-cleaner housing. The camshaft used in the W-30 was aggressive, using 328 degrees of duration and a lift of 0.475 inches. That's a lot of cam for a street car. Carburetion was handled by a Rochester Quadrajet 4-barrel

W-31

Lovers of small-block performance weren't left out in the cold; the W-31 option ($310) offered 325 hp in a no-BS package. Once again, power brakes weren't available due to the lack of sufficient vacuum, which was a result of the radical camshaft. New for 1969 was the availability of an automatic transmission (a modified Turbo Hydra-matic 350) bolted onto the W-31. The twin scoops beneath the front bumper were a subtle tip-off that this wasn't your Grandma's Cutlass. Call-out decals above the front side-marker lights let people at stoplights know what was about to embarrass them.

Magazine Tests

The gang at *Car and Driver* magazine spent some quality time with a new, 500-mile 1969 W-31 and timed a quarter-mile performance of 14.5 seconds at 97.2 mph. The staff gushed over the handling of the car, stating that it was "the best compromise between ride and handling we've ever found in a sedan." It was high praise indeed.

Car Life performed an extensive test on a W-31 and praised it to the moon. "Somebody has taken a heavy car with a mid-range engine and made it perform with super cars. Handling is improved with no sacrifice in ride. Price is competitive with the Salvation-Army interior budget super cars, while the plush lining of the standard Cutlass remains."

In model year 1969, the W-31 sold 913 units (including ragtops), which was an improvement from the year before. Midway through the model year, Oldsmobile released the W-31 in convertible form. However, being that late in the run, only 26 were sold.

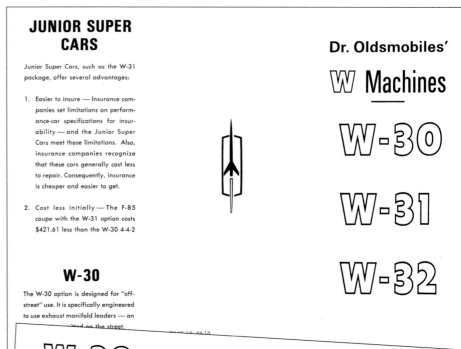

The vast array of W-powered Oldsmobiles was on display in this W-Machines foldout offered by Oldsmobile. The automaker added the W-33 in 1970. (Photo Courtesy General Motors)

Enter the W-32

Yet another W model was available in 1969: the 4-4-2 W-32. This was an interesting melding of choice performance parts cherry-picked to create a superbly roadable package that would scare you on cue. It was a rare model with only 297 built, as it was a midyear release. Only one engine and one transmission were available: the 350-hp 400-ci V-8 bolted to a modified Turbo Hydra-matic 400 automatic transmission. The transmission was calibrated with higher shift points, a higher stall converter, and

From the subtle W-32 decals on the front fender to the trumpet exhaust tips, the 1969 4-4-2 W-32 was intended as a gentleman's express. While the visually extravagant Hurst/ Olds was a head turner, the W-32 rolled beneath the radar.

In model year 1969, only 297 W-32s were built. The option was introduced late in the model year, and when it landed in showrooms, most dealers didn't really understand it. Advertising from Oldsmobile was sparse as well; only one Dr. Oldsmobile ad targeting the W-32 is known to have been used.

Oldsmobile didn't mess around when it came to directing cool air into the 1969 W-32's induction system. The twin flexible tubing could move a lot of air into the dual-snorkel air cleaner housing. Under full throttle, the 400-ci engine needed lots of fresh air and lots of high-octane fuel.

crisper shifting. The camshaft was a milder one than was used in the W-30 with 286 degrees of duration, 0.472-inch lift, and 58 degrees of overlap.

The forced-air induction system was standard on the W-32. Priced at $121.12, the option delivered a lot of technology for the money. A heavy-duty radiator, an anti-spin rear axle, and hood stripes were part of the package. One difference between the W-30 and the W-32 was the change in inner fender liners: the W-32 used black ones.

Oldsmobile performance was well represented in 1969, and the Lansing crowd had big plans for 1970. Customers weren't disappointed.

The vivid interior in this 1969 W-32 used the standard Cutlass pieces. Air-conditioning and a manual transmission was not available in the W-32. This example sports windup windows as well.

The 1969 4-4-2 W-32 used a smooth hood, meaning that it didn't have the functional induction system found on the W-30. Check out the chrome edging of the intake scoops below the turn signals—talk about subtle! In period Dr. Oldsmobile advertisements, this powerplant was referred to as a honker with culture.

The 1969 4-4-2 W-32 wasn't available with many options, but it came from the assembly line with a healthy slate of standard features, such as front disc brakes and a beefy Turbo Hydra-matic 400 3-speed automatic transmission. A long-stroke 400-ci engine was standard as well.

DR. OLDSMOBILE SELLS PERFORMANCE

Oldsmobile marketing got off to a strong start at the Chicago Auto Show for 1969. A fully lettered W-31 sits on display at the event, telling the public about the W-Machines. (Photo Courtesy General Motors)

Selling performance in the late 1960s and early 1970s was a challenging task, and the competition was intense. It wasn't enough for a manufacturer to sell muscle cars that would make a tire store owner a very rich man. The carmakers had to entice buyers into showrooms using advertisements that stretched the bounds of believability, and no company stretched believability like the Dr. Oldsmobile campaign. Oldsmobile headquarters told its dealer network that "W Machines are the IN THING!"

Picture a tall, slender fellow with a turn-of-the-century hairstyle, wearing a white lab coat, surrounded by loyal (if strange) assistants, building over-the-top muscle cars. Add a dash of surrealistic photography reminiscent of an old horror film, boastful ad copy, and unique settings, and you get a taste of the most spectacular set of ads in the entire muscle car era. The cast of characters included Wind Tunnel Waldo, Shifty Sidney, Elephant Engine Ernie, Esses Fernhill, and Hy Spy. These were extravagant productions that hoped to grab a younger demographic.

The division even offered dealerships a $39.95 kit designed to transform a corner of the showroom into a varooom room. Oldsmobile headquarters pitched it as a way to "Attract a Young, New Breed of Enthusiast Buyers to Your Dealership." This package included a plastic chain and a padlock to hold down the W-Machine (as seen in ads), four pylons to delineate the space, a banner with checkered flags designed "to tell prospects where it's at," and various booklets, posters, and Dr. Oldsmobile decals.

Starting with the 1969 model year products, the Dr. Oldsmobile ads ran until the 1971 models. By the end of 1970, the plug was pulled on the campaign, as all of the manufacturers started stepping away from performance. The combination of ramped-up federal emissions regulations along with skyrocketing insurance premiums sent the power output and sales numbers in a steep decline. At that point, the target market shifted, and within a few years, mere transportation was being advertised.

Advertising agency Leo Burnett Co. bought competitor D. P. Brother Co. on March 20, 1967, and part of that package was the Oldsmobile account. Burnett created the Dr. Oldsmobile campaign, which is shown to good effect in this spot, extolling the virtues of the 1969 F-85 W-31. A set of four posters was available by sending $1 to Oldsmobile, P. O. Box W-31 in Plymouth, Michigan. (Photo Courtesy General Motors)

This is another of the Dr. Oldsmobile ads that showed how he and his band of assistants could transform a conventional Oldsmobile into a W-31 W-Machine. Billed as a mini-priced, maxi-powered machine, the W-31 package was value rich, if not a big seller. (Photo Courtesy General Motors)

Hand-picked engine internal parts might seem to be a waste of time in an assembly-line vehicle, but the 1969 W-31 enjoyed that luxury.

Leo Burnett Co., the ad agency behind the Dr. Oldsmobile campaign, created a series of ads that harkened back to vintage horror films to make a series of advertising spots that were unforgettable. (Photo Courtesy General Motors)

DR. OLDSMOBILE SELLS PERFORMANCE *CONTINUED*

An Uncle Fester-esque mascot accompanied the new Dr. Oldsmobile advertising campaigns. (Photo Courtesy General Motors)

IN GRATITUDE TO ALL THOSE WHO HELPED MAKE THE 1970 OLDS 4-4-2 AND W-MACHINES EVERYTHING THEY'RE GOING TO BE.
(namely, fantastic!)

Nobody's more serious about performance than Dr. Oldsmobile. That's why he's scoured the countryside in search of fresh minds and new ideas for 1970.

You're going to love what the good Doc and his performance committee have come up with. 1970 Olds 4-4-2...

■ New 455-cubic-inch V-8. That's as large a V-8 as has ever been bolted into a special-performance production automobile. And it's standard! (Score one for Dr. O!)

■ New high-performance W-25 package, available. Includes fiberglass hood, functional air scoops, special carb, and hood pin locks. Note scoops are far forward for optimum air-grabbing, air-ramming effect.

■ FE-2 suspension, standard. It's the famous one with stabilizer bars *front and rear!* How good is it? Put it this way—the imitators are already popping up faster than you can say "me too."

■ The end of the bump and grind. A super-beefy 3-speed manual with Hurst Competition Shifter, standard. So smooth and positive your kid sister could wing it. Close- or wide-ratio 4-speed or performance-calibrated Turbo Hydra-matic, available.

■ New super-wide tires, standard. G70 fiberglass-belted biggies mounted on 7-inch heavy-duty wheels. (How does that grab you, pavement?)

And that's just a smidgen of what's in store from Olds. For more complete info, specs, and prices, head for your nearest Olds 4-4-2/W-Machine dealer.

Dr. O and Performance Committee: Special merit award to (1) Elephant Engine Ernie for the big 455 V-8. (2) Shifty Sidney for development of the smoothest shifters this side of an automatic. (3) Wind Tunnel Waldo for scientifically placing those whopper scoops way up where they do some good. (4) Esses Fernhill for his tireless testing and perfecting of the FE-2 underpinnings. (5) Hy Spy for keeping an ear to the ground and an eye at the knothole—to keep the good Doc (and you) one jump and a cube or two ahead of competition. (6) Dr. Oldsmobile.

The Dr. Oldsmobile ad campaign was running on all cylinders when this spot for the 1970 4-4-2 and W-Machines graced magazines. This advertisement introduced the entire ensemble that helped the good doctor create the outrageous vehicles found in your local Oldsmobile showroom. (Photo Courtesy General Motors)

1970: Apex Muscle

Everything had been leading up to this. All of the muscle car manufacturers fighting over the performance pie hit their high-water mark almost simultaneously. General Motors lifted its ban on engine displacement in its intermediate platforms, allowing its divisions to shoe-horn monster powerplants between the shock towers.

When it came to huge engines, Oldsmobile was in with both feet. The 455-ci V-8 that had been a fixture in Hurst/Olds vehicles now became a reality for the 4-4-2. The 400-ci engine, long a workhorse in the A-platform, was shown off the stage. Better living through cubic inches.

Looking like an elegant bully, the 1970 4-4-2 W-30 had the perfect amount of attitude, even when sitting still. Riding on a 112-inch wheelbase, it tipped the scales around 3,800 pounds, but with 500 ft-lbs of torque, it could haul down a straight line better than most. It would trip the lights at the drag strip in 13.98 seconds at 100.78 mph.

This is a picture of graceful lines. The sweeping styling of the 1970 4-4-2 W-30 was a handsome blend of restraint and elegance, and it could blur the pavement with the best of them.

The GM A-Body platform was the ideal size for the classic muscle car formula. In SX guise, the 1970 Oldsmobile Cutlass was a graceful example of an executive express. The SX option was frosting on the cake.

This 1970 SX has been retrofitted with a W-25 fiberglass hood. From the factory, the hood would have been a smooth steel item. The SX package was intended to emphasize luxury over sport, as an Oldsmobile marketing bulletin stated that the big-block engine was intended as "a performance engine designed to operate with higher axle ratios."

Oldsmobile offered the latest in audio sophistication in the 1970 Cutlass SX with the installation of the vaunted 8-track tape player. This option was the height of convenience for audiophiles.

Starting life as a 1970 Cutlass Supreme, the SX package was long on mechanical features but shy on flashy exterior ornamentation. Intended to skirt the increasingly tough insurance regulations covering performance cars, the SX didn't sport an identifying VIN that clued the insurance companies in to the powerplant beneath the long hood.

General Motors fitted a cowl tag to the A-Body platform next to the left-side hood hinge. This tag allowed line workers to easily identify the make and model of the vehicle while it still lacked a considerable number of key components.

The engine compartment of the 1970 Cutlass SX looked a lot like a 4-4-2's. That shouldn't be a surprise, as the performance flagship donated a lot of performance goodies for a good cause. A W-32 455-ci engine lurked under the air cleaner. This particular example has a retrofitted cold air induction system; stock W-32s used a smooth hood and closed-style air cleaner.

The steel Rally Sport wheels were wildly popular and very rugged. A chrome trim ring encircled the wheel, and a chromed center cap and bright lug nuts completed the package. Because they were steel, it was affordable enough for the factory to paint them body color. The standard size was G78-14.

If this showed up in the rearview mirror, most people wouldn't pay it any attention. But when it rocketed past at the next stoplight, it had their full attention. Call it a stealth 4-4-2 if you like, but the 1970 SX was a true wolf in sheep clothing—very elegant clothing.

Buyers of 1970 4-4-2 W-30s who wanted to save a little money rode on the base wheel/ tire package. Commonly known as dog-dish hubcaps, they contrasted well with the body-color-painted steel wheels.

This angle of a 1970 4-4-2 W-30 allows us to see the W-27 aluminum differential cover as well as the rear anti-sway bar. The fuel tank between the trumpet-tipped exhaust pipes held 20 gallons of very high-test fuel.

Twilight Blue was a popular color on the 1970 4-4-2 W-30. The spoiler mounted on the trunk (RPO W35) didn't contribute much downforce, but in that era, such a device ramped up the visual aggressiveness, which was important in muscle cars.

W-25 Fiberglass Hood

Change for the Oldsmobile A-platform wasn't limited to under-hood bits; the body was freshened as well. The front grille was cleaned up, and a new hood was fitted. Vehicles wearing the W-30 callouts no longer used a pair of low-slung scoops and flexible tubing to funnel ambient air into the induction system; the new W-25 fiberglass hood incorporated a pair of functional scoops.

Under normal throttle usage, the engine breathed through a pair of snorkels on the air cleaner housing. However, mash the gas pedal to the floor, and a vacuum solenoid opened a flap on the underside of the hood, allowing fresh air to flow from the twin scoops at the front of the hood directly into the top of the air-cleaner assembly.

The rear quarter panels now had a curving, sweeping line that echoed the top fender line. At the rear, new taillights used a pair of vertical lenses on each side of

The 4-4-2 W-30 was offered on a number of Cutlass body types, including the Sport Coupe. With its window frames and B-pillar, it was a stiffer body shell than the Holiday Hardtop.

In 1970, Oldsmobile offered Super Stock III wheels with body-colored centers. Still sized 14x7 inches, they were a striking styling element in the overall look of the 1970 4-4-2 W-30.

the trunk lid within the bumper. A broad stripe ran the length of the car at knee height, and behind the front wheels on the fender within the stripe was where Oldsmobile placed the W-30 graphic.

W-30 Going Strong

The W-30 was icing on the 4-4-2 cake, and it was an elegant bruiser. Front disc brakes were now standard on W-30s, which was handy when the big 455 engine was rated at 370 hp at 5,200 rpm. The standard 4-4-2's 455 engine was advertised at 365 hp at just 5,000 rpm. Torque came in at a stump-pulling 500 ft-lbs at 3,600 rpm, which was enough to hurl the W-30 down a drag strip in 14.2 seconds at 102.14 mph. A compression ratio of 10.5:1 from 80-cc combustion chambers in the *F*-casting heads meant that drivers were looking for premium fuel—and a lot of it. At the time, high-test gasoline cost less than 50 cents a gallon. The exhaust note was pure magic, a snapping crackle mixed with a guttural rumble. It was as if the engine was calling for more throttle.

The dramatic hood scoops on the 1970 4-4-2 W-30 were functional. Ducting on the underside of the hood fed ambient air onto the top of the air cleaner element. The rear decklid spoiler (RPO W35) was a $73 option.

Within the body-length stripe on this 1970 4-4-2 was the W-30 callout that let people know that this was a Big Dog. The G70x14 wheel/tire package looked great, but all those tires were good for was keeping the frame off the ground. What street tire of the day could grip with 500 ft-lbs of torque?

This 1970 4-4-2 W-30 is equipped with 14x7-inch Super Stock I wheels. Goodyear Polyglas tires were cutting-edge rubber in the day. You can only imagine what other tires were like . . . Red inner wheel liners are visible in the wheel well.

Unlike many of its muscle car contemporaries, the 1970 4-4-2 W-30 could actually take a corner pretty well. Fitted with beefy front and rear anti-sway bars, it clung to the pavement while body lean was kept controlled.

Oldsmobile labeled the hood with functional scoops as W-25, and that design proved to be an iconic 4-4-2 feature. At the other end of the car, trumpet exhaust tips were included in the W-30 package.

Looking regal in Tuxedo Black, this 1970 4-42 W-30 convertible shows off its red molded plastic inner fender well liners. With 500 ft-lbs of torque, the resemblance of a 1970 4-4-2 W-30 to a locomotive was not a far stretch of the imagination. Aftermarket radial tires improve both ride and grip.

Painted Oldsmobile blue, this 1970 4-4-2 W-30's 455-ci engine is poised to breathe though the hood-mounted scoop's flange on the underside of the hood. The vacuum actuator in the air cleaner assemble controlled the flap that opened and shut, allowing hood-fed air into the air cleaner housing.

The editors at MotorTrend magazine flogged a 1970 4-4-2 W-30 down a drag strip equipped with a 4-speed manual transmission and 3.39:1 rear axle gears. They recorded a time of 14.2 seconds at 102 mph. It takes a lot of power to get a 2-ton machine to crank out numbers like that.

Oldsmobile called this 1970 color Sebring Yellow; Chevrolet put the same hue on the Corvette and called it Daytona Yellow. No fixation with American racetracks. Oldsmobile built just 96 convertible 1970 4-4-2 W-30s equipped with a 4-speed manual transmission. It's the best of all worlds.

Dual stripes on top of the functional hood scoops were a tasteful nod to racing stripes but with typical Oldsmobile restraint. They worked well with the full-length side body stripe.

Just 264 1970 4-4-2 W-30 convertibles were built out of a total of 2,933 ragtop 4-4-2s. This vehicle is one of the 168 constructed with an automatic transmission.

Rowing the W-30

Transmission choices for the W-30 were straightforward. If your preference was to manually row gears, you got the close-ratio heavy-duty box. Period. Want to work two pedals and let the transmission handle gear choice? Oldsmobile fit the M40 under the transmission hump. This automatic was a strengthened OW Turbo Hydra-matic 400, complete with a high-RPM (between 2,400 and 2,600) stall torque converter, higher shift points, and crisper shifts.

Offered for the first time, RPO W-26 gave a buyer a center console equipped with a lighted map pocket and the famed Hurst Dual Gate shifter. This feature allowed a driver to move the shifter sideways into a secondary gate that gave manual control of gear selection. Atop the W-30 engine, Oldsmobile now used an aluminum intake manifold in an effort to reduce weight. In that same vein, it offered W-27, an aluminum differential carrier and cover, onto the rear axle, which shaved 22 pounds off the scale and added $157.98 to the window sticker. This one-year-only option incorporated a finned aluminum cover, which helped cool the differential fluid temperature by 20 degrees. The W-27's design allowed for an additional pint of fluid capacity compared to regular differentials.

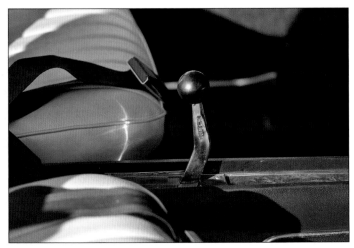

A lot of 1970 4-4-2 W-30 owners picked the beefy Turbo Hydra-matic 400 3-speed automatic transmission as their gearbox of choice. Hurst supplied the shifters on every one of them.

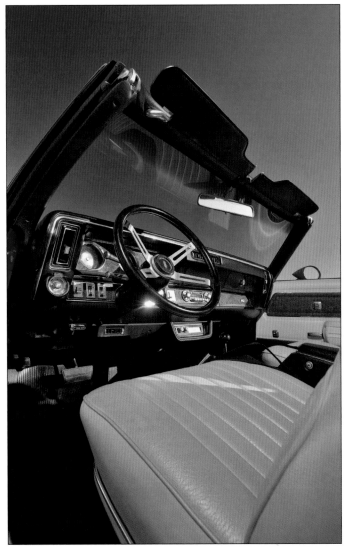

This 1970 4-4-2 W-30 convertible is heavily loaded with options, including power windows, brakes, and steering; an automatic transmission; an 8-track tape player; air-conditioning; and unlimited sunshine. The tasteful four-spoke steering wheel was standard on the 1970 4-4-2 W-30. The tachometer surrounds the clock in the far-right circular instrument recess in a display called a Tic-Toc-Tach display.

The four-element vertical taillights debuted on the Cutlass line in the 1970 model. This 4-4-2 W-30 packed 370 hp under the hood, and those poor G70x14 rear tires didn't stand a chance against a heavy foot.

This was cutting-edge audio in a vehicle in 1970: an AM/FM stereo radio and an 8-track tape player. Simulated burl walnut covered the dashboard from door to door, giving the midsize Oldsmobile an upscale feel.

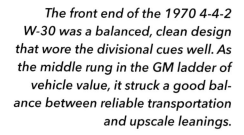

Nicknamed the His & Hers shifter, the Hurst Dual Gate shifter (W-26) allowed a driver to let the transmission shift gears effortlessly, or, by moving the shift lever into a parallel set of detents, each gear could be chosen at the driver's discretion.

The front end of the 1970 4-4-2 W-30 was a balanced, clean design that wore the divisional cues well. As the middle rung in the GM ladder of vehicle value, it struck a good balance between reliable transportation and upscale leanings.

The W-27 aluminum differential cover was a 1970-only component. It was fitted to reduce weight. Besides, it looked great. Note the original spiral rear shock absorber.

Take a Look Inside

The interior of the Metallic Blue W-30 455 engine was filled with solid engineering. Oldsmobile had a program called Select Fit, which meant that items such as the pistons were cherry-picked for the very best quality. An undersquare design with a 4.125-inch bore and a 4.125-inch stroke, it was a simple but durable design.

Oldsmobile performance guru Joe Mondello recounted in *Hemmings Muscle Machines* magazine (August 2005) that compared to other GM engines: "Their engines [Oldsmobile] were better built. Most were hand assembled, and Oldsmobile had A, B, C, and D pistons so that they could be perfectly matched to the bore. All of them were statically balanced, including the pistons, rods, and crankshaft. Olds was a notch above the others."

Oldsmobile had enough confidence in the design and durability of the big engine to build every W-30 engine with two-bolt main bearing caps. The hydraulic valves incorporated positive valve rotators to reduce deposits and improve long-term compression. A performance-tuned Rochester Quadrajet sat atop the aluminum intake manifold. A W-30 using an automatic transmission was fitted with a part number 7040257 carb, while a 4-speed car had a part number 7040253 unit atop the aluminum intake manifold. Fuel mileage with enthusiastic driving was in the single digits, but no one bought a 4-4-2 W-30 to achieve good fuel economy.

What kind of performance could a W-30 driver expect? Thrilling! Launching the car from rest required a deft touch, as the massive torque would overpower any tire. Gently rolling into the throttle off the line, then feeding more gas in as the speed grew was the answer to putting all that power to the ground.

Car Life magazine flogged a 1970 4-4-2 W-30 down a drag strip and ran 14.36 seconds at 100.22 mph. Those were darn good numbers for a car that tipped the scales at 3,740 pounds in convertible form riding on bias-ply tires. In the real world, the 4.4 seconds to vault from 30 to 70 mph translates into great passing ability. All of this fun didn't come cheap; the well-equipped car that *Car Life* tested stickered for $5,016. That was Corvette money. However, no Corvette could seat five comfortably and haul a healthy amount of luggage.

Loaded with desirable options, this 1970 4-4-2 W-30 boasted power windows, air-conditioning, a remote driver-side exterior mirror, passenger-side exterior mirror, shoulder belts, and a Dual Gate shifter in a center console. It also had power to spare.

This control beneath the dashboard of this 1970 4-4-2 W-30 was a T44 hood-locking selector. W-30 engine components were desirable parts. Just saying . . .

The shoulder belts were stored in brackets in the ceiling just inboard from the side windows. Even though the 1970 4-4-2 W-30 was a pure performance car, it was still an Oldsmobile, which meant that it was nicely appointed and well screwed together.

Most people didn't buy 4-4-2 W-30s to listen to the radio. However, an AM unit was standard equipment.

Inset taillights helped protect the lenses in minor bumps. Oldsmobile stylists paid attention to the design details, such as the trunk lip wrapping around the taillights. It was very classy.

The worn paint on this shifter ball shows that this 1970 4-4-2 W-30 has been enjoyed as was intended.

This is not a bad place to hang out. This 1970 4-4-2 W-30 is equipped with a Turbo Hydra-matic 400 3-speed transmission and a Hurst Dual Gate floor-mounted shifter. Note the three sets of seat belts in the back seat, which provide plenty of room to take the whole group.

In this view, you can see the mesh screen affixed to the bottom of the W-25 hood, which was designed to keep rocks and small pets out of the induction system. This particular W-30 is fitted with factory air-conditioning; the large Frigidaire compressor is on the right side of the engine and is driven by an accessory belt. In 1970, all 4-4-2 W-30s were fitted with an aluminum intake manifold at the factory. Beneath the intake manifold were combustion chambers that delivered 10.5:1 compression, which required only high-octane leaded fuel—and lots of it. The Rochester Quadrajet 4-barrel could flow a lot of fuel quickly. As the 1970 4-4-2 W-30 rolled down the assembly line, it was the job of a line worker to fill the vehicle's cooling system with antifreeze, test the mixture, then mark in crayon on the radiator core support what temperature the engine was safe to. In this case, it was -10°F. Changing the spark plugs on the right bank could be a knuckle-skinning job. The big 455-ci engine actually fit well in the engine compartment of the A-Body. The red plastic fender liners were an attempt to cut down on weight, especially over the front tires.

The front end of the 1970 4-4-2 W-30 was a balanced, clean design that wore the divisional cues well. As the middle rung in the GM ladder of vehicle value, it struck a good balance between reliable transportation and upscale leanings. The W-25 fiberglass hood, complete with functional scoops and twist hold-down pins, was a stylish way to put cooler air into the induction system. The waterfall center section of the hood debuted in 1969.

W-31 More Time

Back for its junior year, the W-31 continued being the little small-block terror that it had been in previous years. Newly designed cylinder heads with 2.005/1.630-inch intake/exhaust valves and heavy-duty valve springs purred the engine. Sitting atop the block was an aluminum intake manifold with a 750-cfm Rochester Quadrajet glistening above. All of this sat below the new W-25 hood, which gulped air into a low-restriction air cleaner assembly.

The final tally for 1971 saw 1,029 Cutlass S Holiday Coupes, 116 Sport Coupes, and 207 F-85s traversing Oldsmobile assembly lines.

A superb design, the 1970 W-31 used small callouts on the front fenders to alert other drivers that a little stoplight challenge might not be a good idea. With 360 ft-lbs of torque, the biggest worry was getting the rear tires to grip. But the 350-ci engine was to rev; peak horsepower (325) was reached at 5,400 rpm.

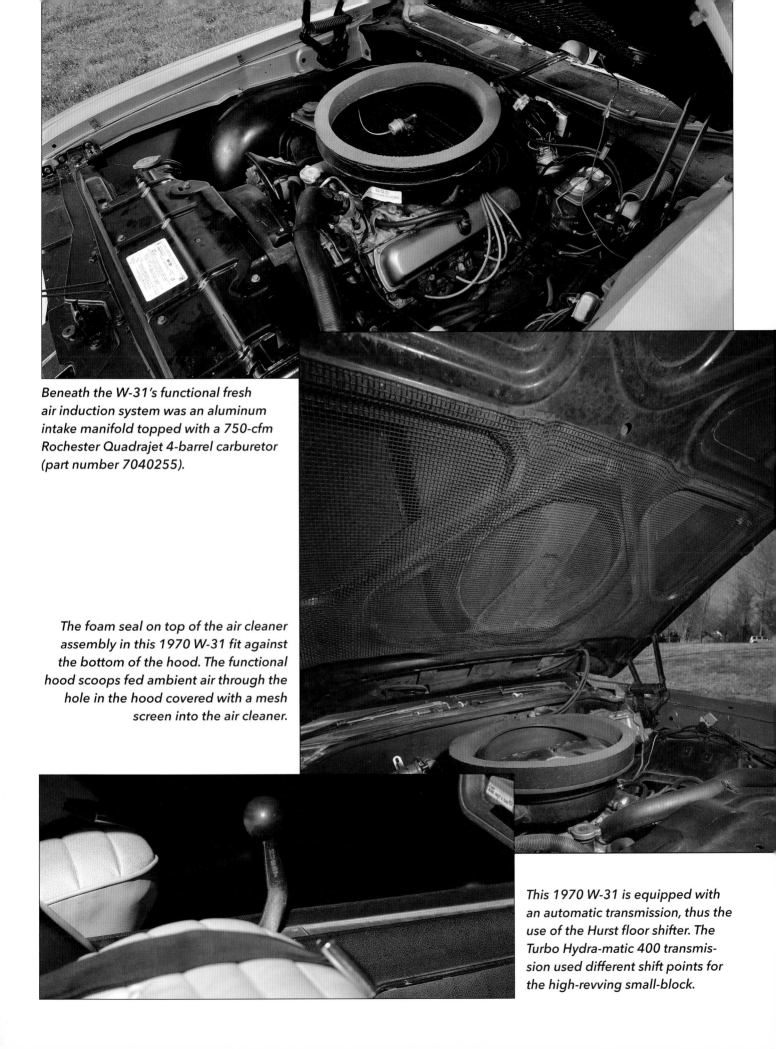

Beneath the W-31's functional fresh air induction system was an aluminum intake manifold topped with a 750-cfm Rochester Quadrajet 4-barrel carburetor (part number 7040255).

The foam seal on top of the air cleaner assembly in this 1970 W-31 fit against the bottom of the hood. The functional hood scoops fed ambient air through the hole in the hood covered with a mesh screen into the air cleaner.

This 1970 W-31 is equipped with an automatic transmission, thus the use of the Hurst floor shifter. The Turbo Hydra-matic 400 transmission used different shift points for the high-revving small-block.

The final year of W-31 production was 1970, and only 1,352 were built. The standard rear-axle ratio was the 3.91:1 limited-slip unit, which was ideal for getting the high revs onto the ground.

Oldsmobile didn't go for huge graphics on the W-31 models; it preferred to let the performance do the talking. Big brother W-30 got most of the ink in enthusiast magazines and most of the sales. Weak sales numbers were a primary reason that the W-31 option was pulled after three years in production.

Twist hood-locking pins were part of the fiberglass W-25 hood, and unlike many factory attempts to secure the hood with a racing-inspired setup, the Oldsmobile solution actually worked well.

The interior of the 1970 W-31 was essentially a regular Cutlass, which is a pretty good place to be. This particular car is equipped with the Dual Gate floor shifter for its automatic transmission.

From the rear, a 1970 W-31 looked like a regular Oldsmobile Cutlass. The exhaust was raspy and threatening, but visually, this muscle car was a wolf in sheep's clothing.

PACING *THE* RACE

The total package wasn't lost on the folks at the Indianapolis Motor Speedway. The 1970 Oldsmobile 4-4-2 was picked to pace the Greatest Spectacle in Racing. Former race winner Rodger Ward piloted the graceful Oldsmobile convertible around the storied track, resplendent in its Porcelain White finish and vinyl stripes.

Equipped with an automatic transmission, it had no problem sustaining the triple-digit speed needed to lead the pack. Oldsmobile installed a set of Vista Cruiser rear drum brakes to help scrub speed off on the track. As was the practice, Oldsmobile made replicas of the pace car available for sale at dealers; a total of 626 were built with a Y-74 code on the cowl tag. The breakdown of that number included 358 Cutlass Supremes and 268 4-4-2s. Race winner Al Unser received a Festival Car as part of the winner's package. That car is now on display at the Unser Museum in Albuquerque, New Mexico.

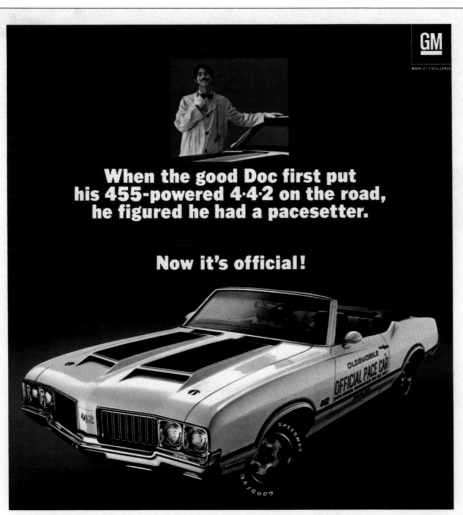

When the good Doc first put his 455-powered 4-4-2 on the road, he figured he had a pacesetter.

Now it's official!

The motion-minded folks at Indy have just named 4-4-2 the official pace car for this year's classic.

It's easy to see why. Its standard V-8 has a pace-setting 455-cu.-in. displacement. Nobody in its class offers more. Its valve system is revolutionary, featuring positive valve rotators for more efficient performance, longer engine life. Its special suspension with front and rear stabilizers? Fast becoming the most imitated in the business.

Ready to set a pace of your own? See your Olds dealer and test-drive a 4-4-2 or other Olds. You'll find that great performance runs in the family.

OLDS 4-4-2 SPECS

Engine type	H.C. Rocket V-8
Displacement	455 cu. in.
Bhp	365 at 5000 rpm
Torque, lb.-ft.	500 at 3200 rpm
Bore x stroke, in.	4.125 x 4.250
Compression ratio	10.50-to-1
Combustion chamber volume, min. allowable	91.72 cc
Min. cyl. head vol.	69.75 cc
Min. deck clearance	.002 below
Carburetion	Quadrajet 4-bbl
Camshaft duration Intake/exhaust (Sync)	294°/296°
Camshaft overlap Intake/exhaust (Sync)	68°
Total valve lift Intake/exhaust	.472
Valve diameter (Max.) Intake	2.077
Exhaust	1.630
Brakes	9.5" drums
Transmission	Full sync h-d 3-on-the-floor, Hurst Competition Shifter
Axle (Sync)	3.08 ratio
Exhaust system	Full duals
Suspension	FE2
Has h-d springs, shocks, rear control arms, plus stabilizer bars front and rear	
Wheels	H-d 14" with 7" rim
Tires	G70
bias-belted with white stripe	
Strato Bucket Seats	Std.
Lightweight fiberglass hood, functional scoops, big hood stripes, chromed hood tie-downs, and low-restriction air cleaner (W25), available.	

Oldsmobile 4·4·2

Because the 1970 4-4-2 W-30 used such an aggressive camshaft (296-degree duration), power brakes were not available, as the vehicle was equipped with a manual transmission. At low RPM, the engine didn't generate enough vacuum to operate a power brake booster. Disc brakes in the front (10.9 inches) were standard, and while they performed better than drum brakes, stopping distances were nowhere near what we enjoy today. Bringing the car to a halt from 80 mph took 325 feet. We're talking football-field length.

The 1970 model year 4-4-2 led the charge at the Indianapolis 500-Mile Race. Before the division folded, it provided pace cars for 11 races. Buyers could walk into a 1970 Oldsmobile dealership and drive out in a track-ready A-Body. At least, that's what this ad spot was selling. (Photo Courtesy General Motors)

W-45: RALLYE 350

The year 1970 was the apogee of performance in the American muscle car universe. Vehicle manufacturers that traditionally eschewed sheer velocity as being beneath them had seen that younger buyers were spending serious money on vehicles that could lay waste to a set of rear tires without breaking a sweat. At Oldsmobile, the 4-4-2 W-30 was the alpha of the lineup, and that level of performance wasn't something that everyone could afford. Customers with slimmer wallets wanted a piece of Oldsmobile performance, and the product planners at the division released a Cutlass model that dished up a good level of grunt mixed with a visual presence that few cars could rival: RPO W-45.

The Rallye 350 was introduced deep in the model year on February 18, 1970. This option was available on any 1970 F-85 Cutlass or Cutlass S two-door hardtop pillared coupe. The price of the option (just $157.98) was an absolute bargain. Buyers could get it in any color, as long as it was Sebring Yellow. And there was no shortage of the hue; it looked like the car had been dipped in a vat of retina-burning paint. The front grilles were blacked out to contrast with the vivid finish. Not only were the body panels sprayed but also the bumpers and N66 14x7-inch Super Stock II wheels wore the color too.

Wrapped around the steel wheels were G70x14 tires. Filched from the 4-4-2 W-30 was the W-25 fiberglass hood that was topped with a pair of black stripes. At the other end, the W-35 trunk-mounted rear spoiler was bolted on. Vinyl graphics on the rear fenders wore *Rallye 350*, and a unique black stripe wrapped over the rear window and flowed toward the rear corners. The body-colored bumpers used a three-stage primer-urethane-color process. The urethane was baked at 250 degrees before the color was applied.

Beneath the long hood was an L74 350-ci V-8 that was topped with a Rochester 4MV 4-barrel carburetor on an iron intake manifold and rated at 310 hp and 390 ft-lbs of torque. Bolted to the back of the engine block could be a 3-speed manual, 4-speed manual, or the M38 Turbo Hydra-matic 350 3-speed automatic transmission. Shifting duties were handled by a column shifter standard, and Hurst floor-mounted units were available as options. The standard gearset in the 12-bolt differential was 3.23:1, although 3.42 and 3.91 gears were available. Underpinnings were beefy thanks to the standard FE2 suspension. That package included front and rear anti-sway bars (0.937-inch front, 0.875-inch rear), stiffer springs (150 in-lbs), and firmer shock absorbers. The exhaust setup was the well-regarded N10 dual system. Performance was brisk with quarter-mile times in the 15-second/94-mph range. It would surge to 60 mph in 7.7 seconds and to 80 mph in 12.1 (*MotorTrend* February 1970).

Built to circumvent the increasingly stiff insurance premiums aimed at performance car owners, the W-45 had nothing in the vehicle identification number (VIN) to show that it had leanings toward muscle. Production figures show that the one-year-only offering was relatively well received. Oldsmobile built a total of 3,547 Rallye 350s with an interesting breakdown on models. The F-85 line had 1,020 transformed into W-45s, while 2,367 Cutlass S hardtop coupes were built. Rarest of them all was the pillared F-85 Sport Coupes with just 160 manufactured.

The 1970 Rallye 350 was not a threat to W-30s, but it combined affordability, enthusiastic performance, and standout visuals to fill a void in a niche in the muscle car field that most manufacturers overlooked. It was a worthy entry in the W-World.

Introduced in February 1970, the Rallye 350 was originally intended to be a Hurst/Olds model, but the product planners at Oldsmobile thought that by offering an entry-level A-Body performance car, they could bring buyers into the Oldsmobile camp with hopes that future purchases would continue to wear the Oldsmobile emblem.

The foam seal atop the air cleaner assembly mated with the bottom of the W-25 Force-Air hood. Rated at 310 hp, the W-45 option package (Rallye 350) was insurance friendly, which was a growing issue in 1970. The 4-4-2 W-30 generated very impressive levels of power, which the insurance companies were closely watching with the inevitable increase in premiums.

Looking as if it had been dipped in a vat of Sebring Yellow Magic Mirror acrylic lacquer, the tasteful use of brightwork created a vehicle with a strong visual presence. Riding on the highly desirable FE2 Rallye Sport Suspension, the Rallye 350 could handle the curves better than most performance cars. Having less weight on the front tires due to the use of the 350-ci engine improved the car's road manners considerably. Late in the production run, Oldsmobile allowed the W27 aluminum differential housing and cover to be fitted to the Rallye 350.

At a time when any performance worth owning used graphics to stand out from the crowd, the one-year-only 1970 Rallye 350 showed restraint, laying down stripes upon the Sebring Yellow paint. Wrapping across the top of the rear window, a two-tone stripe flowed down to the ends of the rear bumper, creating a graceful line. The hood stripes tastefully echoed the treatment.

Wearing the W-35 rear spoiler fitted to every Rallye 350, the "budget" muscle car could cover the quarter-mile in the 15-second range at 94 mph. Because of the car's late model-year introduction, very few were ordered by customers; most were ordered by dealers who then had to try to sell the car to uninformed buyers. Only 3,547 Rallye 350s were built.

This Rallye 350 began life as a Cutlass S, and that means the interior was comfortable. Options such as air conditioning, power windows, door locks, and a power driver's seat were some of the goodies that could be fitted. Even a power trunk release could be installed.

W-33 Full-Size Hot Rodding

As we've seen, the *W* treatment wasn't limited to A-Body Oldsmobiles; the Toronado benefited from the additional power and status that came with the potent prefix. Another vehicle in the catalog of 1970 Oldsmobiles was the recipient of the *W*: the Delta 88 W-33. I know, the combination is incongruous, but the result was a road-going Q-ship—a vehicle that most people wouldn't give a first look at, much less a second look. But what worked in the 4-4-2 worked in the big B-Body Delta 88.

Targeted at government duty, RPO B07 put the kind of beefy underpinnings under the vehicle that were needed for police to chase down perps. The option was designed by then-Assistant Experimental Engineer Ted Louckes.

With one look at the stats, you can tell that this vehicle was designed to be a serious road machine. Front spring rates were stiffened from 335 to 560 in-lbs, while the rear coils went from 125 to 260 in-lbs. Front and rear anti-roll bars were fitted: 1.08 inches in the front, 0.88 inches aft. The California Highway Patrol used these Delmont 88s in their fleet in 1967, continuing a line of Oldsmobile usage in law enforcement dating back into the 1950s.

The package that was to be known as the W-33 was introduced in 1968 as part of the Police Interceptor package. With the introduction of a restyled B-Body for 1968, Oldsmobile felt that it had a viable new entry into the competition for a law enforcement. A heavy-duty frame, heavy-duty springs and shocks, and a strengthened automatic transmission kept the rubber on the road. Propelling the

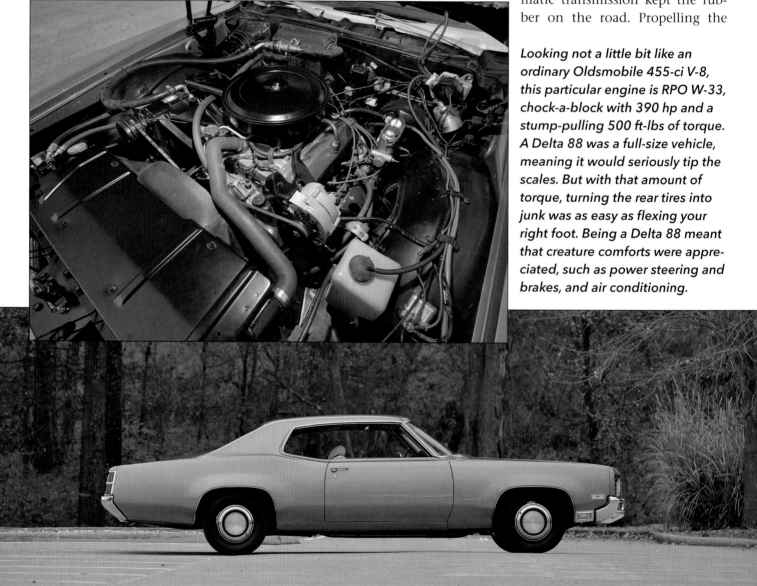

Looking not a little bit like an ordinary Oldsmobile 455-ci V-8, this particular engine is RPO W-33, chock-a-block with 390 hp and a stump-pulling 500 ft-lbs of torque. A Delta 88 was a full-size vehicle, meaning it would seriously tip the scales. But with that amount of torque, turning the rear tires into junk was as easy as flexing your right foot. Being a Delta 88 meant that creature comforts were appreciated, such as power steering and brakes, and air conditioning.

It comes down to proportions. The 1970 Oldsmobile Delta 88 W-33 had superb proportions. The flowing roof line, the amount of front and rear overhang, and the judicious use of chrome and bright trim created broad-shouldered shape that exuded confidence without being ostentatious. Famed General Motors Styling Chief Harley Earl said that the mark of a good designer was knowing when to lift the pen. Here is exhibit A.

Looking not a little bit like a stylish locomotive, the Delta 88 W-33 was a glamorous steam roller. In the 1960s and early 1970s, full-sized American cars were amply scaled to waft down the interstate highway system like a mechanical cloud. The W-33 option put a considerable amount of sport beneath the vast expanse of sheet metal. Peeking out under the rear axle is the beefy anti-roll bar, which is useful for reducing the big car's body roll during a spirited turn.

it in an advertisement for Oldsmobile. He said it was "the greatest American car I've driven since 1960. Though I have driven others [police cars], this Olds . . . must be rated tops . . . one of the three really great cars I've tested in the last 22 years . . . its superiority is not its speed or its 390-hp engine but its roadability. What an advantage the cops have with these rigs whipping in and out or reaching high speeds in an eyeblink. California and Missouri are using the Olds for police work. In these states, don't try to outrun the cops because they can eat you alive."

hefty Delta 88 was a massaged 455-ci engine rated at 390 hp. In 1968/1969, the engine was fitted with the big-valve C heads. This engine was sourced from the Hurst/Olds, and with 500 ft-lbs of torque, the rear tires tended to live short, violent lives.

Noted *Popular Mechanics* vehicle tester Tom McCahill spent time behind the wheel of the 1968 Oldsmobile Apprehender and had nothing but lavish praise for

One of the requirements that the CHP put upon manufacturers was that the vehicle had to be able to maintain 125 mph in 120-degree heat. The California Highway Patrol used the big Oldsmobile for just one year and then moved to Mopar products. CHP officers weren't exactly in love with the big Oldsmobile, and the department stepped away from them for 1968. Lessons learned from developing the police package were seen in the next few years.

Most dealers had no idea that the upgraded equipment was available, as Oldsmobile headquarters were intent on putting the potent package into the hands of law enforcement. Hence in 1968 and 1969, the setup was known as the Police Pursuit. It wasn't until 1970 that the

The rear fender kick-up at the shoulder line on the 1970 Delta 88 W-33 is reminiscent of the same treatment on the Oldsmobile Toronado. The Delta's graceful and formal lines fit into the General Motors hierarchy of vehicle brands. Oldsmobile fit into the middle of the product ladder, and the timeless style strongly referenced upscale Buick and Cadillac.

W33: FULL-SIZED MUSCLE *by Jerry Wilson*

Oldsmobile provided a wide array of W-Machines during the 1970 model year.

RPO	Function	Production Numbers
W-30	High-performance option for 442	3,090
W-31	High-performance option for F85 and Cutlass	1,352
W-32	High-performance option for Cutlass Supreme SX	852
W-33	Highway Patrol option for Delta 88	1,607
W-34	High-performance option for Toronado	5,341

The high-performance engines in the A-Bodies (W-30 in the 442, W-32 in the Cutlass Supreme SX, and W-31 in the Cutlass F85) are well-known and have been in great demand among collectors. However, the high-performance options for the larger Oldsmobiles are not as well-known. The standard engine in the Toronado had 375 hp, and the high-performance-option W-34 provided 400 hp.

The model that has not drawn as much attention is the Oldsmobile B-Body that included the Delta 88 and 98 series. The W-33 option was offered only on the three Delta 88 series:

Series	Body Description	Body Code	Production Numbers
Delta 88 (5400)			541
	Holiday Coupe	5437	
	Holiday Sedan	5439	
	Convertible	5467	
	Town Sedan	5469	
Delta 88 Custom (6400)			518
	Holiday Coupe	6437	
	Holiday Sedan	6439	
	Town Sedan	6469	
Delta 88 Royale (6600)			548
	Holiday Coupe	6647	

The W33 option includes a high-performance 455-ci engine with 390 hp and required a heavy-duty Turbo Hydra-matic 400 transmission (designated OL, Option M41). Many Delta 88s with the W-33 option were ordered by state highway patrols. In Southern California, these were known as "Freeway Flyers." Other options offered for highway patrol use in 1970 included:

Option	Code
Heavy-Duty Engine Cooling and 55 Ampere Delcotron	Y72
Heavy-Duty Frame	F35
Automatic Transmission Oil Cooling Auxiliary	M55
Highway Patrol Suspension	B07
Heavy-Duty Front Disc Brakes (Includes N99)	J55
Heavy-Duty Wheels	N99
Police Speedometer Certified	U11
Black Vinyl Front and Rear Floor Covering (four-door only)	BG1
Wiring Harness for Roof Flasher	U90

Note: In 1968 and 1969, the 390-hp 455 was designated as option L32 and was mated with a Turbo Hydra-matic 400 (designated OL, Option M41 in 1969). There was no M41 listed in the available options for 1968. However, transmission Option M41 was offered in 1966 and 1967. There is a reference to a 1968 Option W-33, but that is not on the option list published by Oldsmobile.

engine was denoted *W-33*. Checking the box on the order form put the engine in the car, but it didn't include any other modifications. Listed on the window sticker for $77.94, it was one of the era's performance steals.

Examples in 1970 used the 2.07-inch intake *E* heads. Buyers in the know could further upgrade the mechanicals by ordering RPO B07 Police package, giving the big Delta 88 a heavy-duty suspension, a heavy-duty automatic transmission, and a boxed frame to increase structural rigidity. The Turbo Hydra-matic 400 M41 transmission was a mandatory option and cost a whopping $242.88!

Sales of the 1970 Delta 88 W-33 wasn't exactly stellar with just 1,607 units: 541 Delta 88s, 518 Delta 88 Customs, and 548 Delta 88 Royales. With such low numbers, Oldsmobile felt that modifying the engine to meet 1971

In 1970, this was luxury—Oldsmobile style! The faux-wood trim, reaching across the entire dashboard and inserted into the door panels, was a stylish touch that wasn't found in traditional muscle cars. By 1970, insurance companies were coming down hard on buyers of performance cars, and the Cutlass SX was a low-key cruiser that happened to have the heart of a 4-4-2.

Every Cutlass SX came with a Turbo Hydra-matic automatic transmission controlled by a Hurst Dual Gate shifter. George Hurst revolutionized the transmission shifter market and went on to invent the Jaws of Life hydraulic rescue tool.

Few muscle cars of the day could boast both luxury and performance while maintaining aggressive and sleek styling. The SX checked both boxes.

From this angle, the 1970 Cutlass SX could be mistaken for a run-of-the-mill Cutlass. As one of the top-selling vehicles in America in 1970, the Cutlass was seen everywhere, and most people weren't aware of how potent the SX version was. One stoplight encounter could change that.

emissions standards wasn't cost effective. Thus, the plug was pulled.

Production numbers showed that the love of performance was still rampant. Oldsmobile put 262 Sport Coupes, 2,574 Holiday Coupes, and 264 convertible W-30s into good homes. The total of 3,100 was an increase over the prior year. Yet, changes were coming that would transform the muscle car field from a stoplight bully to a pale shadow. Like all domestic auto manufacturers, Oldsmobile felt the cold wind blow in, cooling the performance car flame almost into oblivion. There were forces at work that would change the entire automotive landscape, and Oldsmobile was not exempt.

Cutlass SX: The *S* Might Have Meant *Stealthy*

As the 1960s drew to a close, performance cars ruled the streets. Affordable, stylish, and brimming with fun, they started to attract the wrong kind of attention from insurance companies. Monthly premiums began increasing to the point where owning a muscle car was economically unfeasible. That in turn affected sales.

Oldsmobile, like every other manufacturer, wanted the performance train to roll as long as possible. It hit upon an idea that allowed buyers to equip an A-Body Cutlass with performance but keep a lower profile than a 4-4-2: the Cutlass Supreme SX, RPO Y79.

The concept was simple. Take a 1970 4-4-2 and pull

A tiny metal SX badge was fitted to each front fender and was the only external indication of its unique build. Oldsmobile used the more expensive badge rather than a decal as a sign of the vehicle's upscale leanings.

off every visual identifying badge, graphic, and hood scoop. The SX model was offered on two Cutlass models: the convertible and the Holiday Sports Coupe. Externally, the exhaust cutouts in the rear bumper were retained, and a pair of discrete SX badges were fitted to the front fenders behind the front wheels. That was the extent of visual cues. Unless you knew what you were looking for, it was very easy to mistake it for the Cutlass your Aunt Elaine drove. Even the VIN was stealthy; there was noth-

The stylists at Oldsmobile really got the front-end design of the 1970 Cutlass SX right. The fiberglass hood with built-in locking twist pins and functional forced-air induction was borrowed from the W-30, and with the contrasting stripes, it struck a balance between sport and subtlety.

1970 model year, Oldsmobile offered two engines in the SX, and both were 455-ci bruisers. The standard powerplant in the beginning of the 1970 production run was the L33, and its 2-barrel carburetor delivered 320 hp and 500 ft-lbs of torque, which continued a trend set by the Turnpike Cruisers from earlier years. It used a rear axle ratio (2.56:1) that emphasized low-RPM cruising rather than brute strength. Later in the year, the L33 was replaced with the L31 powerplant. This engine from the Delta 88 was topped with a 4-barrel carburetor and was advertised as churning out 365 hp.

ing in the VIN to tip off insurance companies that this was not a mainstream Cutlass Supreme.

There were a few caveats that ordering a Cutlass Supreme SX demanded. No manual transmission was available; it was strictly Turbo Hydra-matic time. In the

An optional engine was offered for the entire 1970 model year, and it too was a 455-ci V-8. It was called the

Because all Cutlass SXs used an automatic transmission, a center console was part of the package. The sport steering wheel was one of the best General Motors ever used in a vehicle. Full instrumentation, including a tachometer, was included.

The rear bumper on the 1971 4-4-2 was an elegant design with cutouts for the exhaust tips and recessed taillights. Resisting bumps? Not so much.

The option code for the 1970 Cutlass SX was Y-79, and the result was one heck of a luxurious sleeper. The body-color Rally Sport wheels were a superb stylistic element. Only available in 1970-1971, the SX was a low-selling model that most dealerships didn't know how to market.

W-32 and was the base engine in the 4-4-2. Rated at 365 hp, it used a camshaft that generated its power at higher RPM than the base SX engine. Approximately 1,025 SXs were equipped with the W-32 powerplant in 1970.

Although the Cutlass Supreme SX only used an automatic transmission, the programing between the base engine's use and the W-32's use was different. Turbo Hydra-matics that sat behind a W-32 engine had crisper shifts and carried the same OG transmission code that was standard on the 4-4-2. Inside the car, the transmission shifter was floor-mounted if a console was ordered; otherwise, a column shifter was installed.

Underpinnings were essentially 4-4-2, meaning the Cutlass Supreme SX could handle curves as well as straights. Oldsmobile didn't go overboard in promoting the SX. Remember, it was trying to stay off the insurance company's radar. Sales in 1970 weren't overwhelming, but they were respectable: 7,197 total built (6,404 coupes and 793 ragtops).

Model year 1971 saw the return of the Cutlass Supreme SX, but due to the debut of reduced power, the Big Dog W-32 option was history. Only one engine was now on the roster: the 455 4-barrel known as the L33. With its 8.5:1 compression ratio, the engine was rated at 320 hp and 370 ft-lbs of torque. Sales dropped too, with a total of 2,177 SXs built. That total was divided up as 1,820 coupes and 357 convertibles.

Oldsmobile made the effort to get performance into the hands of anyone who wanted or needed it. The resulting Cutlass Supreme SX was a superb gentleman's hot rod and a sleeper of the first order. Today, they are starting to get the overdue attention they deserve.

1971: Performance Plateau

Enthusiasts entering an Oldsmobile dealership to check out the new 1971 4-4-2 models got a surprise; the cars didn't really look any different than the 1970 cars. The front grille inserts were changed with circular front parking lights replacing the rectangular units of 1970. The taillights were also changed and were now twin horizontal affairs within the bumper. Granted, the Sport Coupe body with its B-pillar was gone.

Looking at the sales brochure, potential buyers would have noticed an omission: the W-31 option. New vehicle emissions regulations were coming down, and the W-31

For the 1971 model year, the entire Cutlass line saw the taillights change from vertical elements to horizontal. Engine compression for the 4-4-2 W-30 was reduced to 8.5:1, taking some of the snap off the car's brutish performance. The cast-iron differential now used an aluminum cover.

couldn't pass. So, it was gone. The brochures listed the power output of the 1971 models, and it looked far lower than the year before. The reason was that manufacturers were starting to list engine power with all the accessories attached, giving net readings.

Yet another indicator of the direction of factory performance was seen in the fine print: engine compression ratios. In 1970, the 4-4-2 W-30's big 455-ci engine packed a 10.5:1 ratio and a thirst for very high-octane fuel. For 1971, the same engine was now using an 8.5:1 compression ratio, two full points lower. The reason was vehicle emissions.

Air quality in America had been steadily declining for many years, and automobiles were one of the major contributors of airborne pollution. The federal government put regulations in place to cut down on vehicular pollution by implementing the widespread adoption of no-lead fuel starting in 1974. With the removal of lead in motor fuel, its octane-boosting and valve-lubricating properties were gone, and manufacturers had to lower compression ratios to allow the vehicles to run on the fuel that was going to be the only one available.

General Motors made a decision that starting in 1971, all of its cars would be able to run on regular-grade leaded fuel. High compression ratios don't like regular fuel. The answer to that was to lower the compression. Tuning the Rochester 4MC carburetor in your garage was

now frowned upon; the factory fitted plastic caps over the idle mixture screws.

As a result, the 1971 Oldsmobile 4-4-2 was now advertised as possessing 340 hp (gross) at 4,600 rpm and 460 ft-lbs of torque at 3,200 rpm. The beloved W-30 version saw 350 hp at 4,700 rpm, while its torque was identical to the regular 4-4-2. A milder camshaft was used, but it didn't adversely affect performance.

Torque rules on the street, and the 1971 W-30 had it in spades. In the May 1971 issue of *Road Test* magazine, the editors wrung out a 4-4-2, covering the quarter-mile in 15.2 seconds at 99 mph. A W-30 would have shaved a couple of tenths off that time, giving a respectable performance. *MotorTrend* used its October 1970 issue to flog a W-30 4-speed prototype, recording a 0-60 mph time of 6.6 seconds. Another run in a W-30 with an automatic gave a 6.1-second vault to 60 mph. The hot shoes at *MotorTrend* coaxed a quarter-mile time of 14.4 seconds at 97 mph. Unchanged was the superb suspension, accurate steering, and upscale fit and finish. Customers getting cars equipped with a manual transmission could order a dual-disc clutch; it was the smart call.

Sales of the 4-4-2 W-30 didn't approach prior years, as the insurance companies were starting to crack down on performance cars. Oldsmobile built just 920 for model year 1971: 810 hardtop coupes and 110 convertibles. Unbeknownst to buyers, this was the last year for a stand-alone 4-4-2. Starting in 1972, the nameplate became an appearance and handling option (W-29) for the Cutlass and Cutlass Supreme. The end of W performance was very near.

1972: Pressing On, Regardless

What a difference two years can make. The 1970 4-4-2 W-30 was one of the most-feared muscle cars on the road—an elegant weapon of speed. The 1972 4-4-2 became an option package for the Cutlass Coupe and Cutlass Supreme convertible, and the W-30 was now an optional feature only available if the 4-4-2 handling and appearance package was ordered. For 1972, the 4-4-2 package (W-29) could be ordered on a Cutlass Hardtop Coupe, Cutlass S Sports Coupe, Cutlass S Hardtop Coupe, or Cutlass Supreme Convertible. The Sports Coupe (post) returned in 1972.

W-30 Power and Transmission Options

The horsepower rating of the 4-4-2 W-30 was just 300 net, while the standard 4-4-2 churned out 270 hp. Underpinnings were still stout, the FE2 ladling on the heavy-duty bits, including front and rear sway bars, heavy-duty springs and shocks, and boxed lower rear control arms. As before, ordering the W-30 gave you the fiberglass hood with functional scoops, the heavy-duty cooling system, and dual exhausts. The engine was still blueprinted at the

The taillights of the 1971 4-4-2 W-30 were horizontal for the first time. This car is equipped with the optional bumper guards. Their thin profile and vertical positioning cast doubt as to their effectiveness.

Power steering and brakes were very useful in allowing a 4-4-2 W-30 to be used as everyday transportation. For many buyers, this was their only car, and it was used in all kinds of driving conditions, from warm sunny days to snow-filled gloom.

Even with optional air-conditioning, power steering, and power brakes, there was still plenty of room in the engine bay of a 1971 4-4-2 W-30. The air-conditioning system used refrigerant R12, which was very effective at cooling the interior.

factory. However, the red fender wells disappeared. The W-30 continued to be a torque monster with 410 ft-lbs of torque. Cubic inches have their advantages.

Transmission choices were easy: the M40 Turbo Hydra-matic 3-speed automatic partnered with a 3.42:1 rear axle ratio or the M20 wide-ratio 4-speed manual, again with the 3.42:1 rear axle ratio. The 455-ci engine was slowly being emasculated, as lower compression and ever more stringent emissions regulations choked the fun out of the engine. Camshafts were different in the W-30 engine depending on the transmission; lift had been reduced to 0.474/0.472-inch when using an automatic transmission and 0.472/0.472-inches with the manual transmission.

Anyone wanting to buy a 4-4-2 W-30 in California was out of luck; the state's harsh emissions regulations shut the door on this model. Oldsmobile Cutlass and Cutlass Supreme convertible buyers who wanted the look of the 4-4-2 without that pesky horsepower could spring for the W-29 option. Called the 4-4-2 Appearance and Handling Package, it equipped any 1972 Oldsmobile A-Body with the look of the top-dog Oldsmobile, including the fiberglass hood, firmer springs and shocks, unique badging, stripes and louvers, as well as boxed-in rear lower control arms. A Cutlass with a 350-ci engine could look the part! As we will see, this was a path every muscle car manufacturer was forced to go down with predictable results.

Once again, Oldsmobile found itself at the front of the pack at the

Indianapolis Motor Speedway, pacing the 1972 race. But this time, it was a Hurst/Olds. The reason for this was interesting; after the debacle of 1971 when the pace car of the Indy 500 crashed into a media tower at the end of the pit row, no manufacturer wanted to go near the race for 1972. Doc Watson and Hurst volunteered to provide a pace car—a Hurst/Olds. Two versions of the 455 engine were available in the 500 Pace Car replica with either the standard 270-hp 4-4-2 engine or the 300-hp W-30 powerplant. Not many of the higher-horsepower versions were built, but regardless of powerplant, they all had Turbo Hydra-matic 3-speed automatic transmis-

sions fitted with Hurst Dual Gate shifters. But the exposure didn't translate into big-block sales.

W-30 Gone for Now but Not Forgotten

Oldsmobile advertising copywriters now stressed the handling ability of the 1972 4-4-2 rather than the vehicle's straight-line performance. The 4-4-2 and W-30 had always been among the top handling cars in the entire segment, and with the shift away from raw performance, the emphasis was away from the weakening powerplants. Now the division was boasting how anyone could drive a 4-4-2 look-alike.

To the surprise of few, sales of the W-30 plummeted, with Oldsmobile selling just 772 for model year 1972: 659 Holiday Coupes and 113 convertibles. The majority of them were equipped with automatic transmissions, as only 289 Holiday Coupes and 33 convertibles employed 4-speed manuals. The path was clear. It was time to pull the plug.

A new body shell was being introduced for the 1973 line. Originally, this new body was intended to be released for the 1972 model year, but there was a financial crunch and the release of the body was pushed back a year. Rather than try to certify the W-30 engine for a diminishing market, Oldsmobile ceased production of the W-30 at the conclusion of the 1972 model year. It went out with a whimper.

Because it was the last year for the second-generation Cutlass offerings, the 1972 model year had Oldsmobile dealers selling 4-4-2s in a wide range of levels. Buyers could go home in a 4-4-2 equipped with a 2-barrel 350-ci V-8 or order higher on the food chain all the way to a W-30 package, complete with 455 muscle.

**Meet the 1972 Olds
4•4•2, 4•4•2, 4•4•2, 4•4•2!**

GM
MARK OF EXCELLENCE

Now you can get 4-4-2 four great ways. And that includes a new, low-priced way! (You're welcome.)

How can we do it? Easy. We've come up with a great new 4-4-2 Sport/Handling Package. And you can order it on four Cutlass models—the Cutlass Supreme Convert, way back there. The Cutlass Hardtop and Cutlass S Coupe, next in line. And that gorgeous Cutlass S Hardtop, front and center. All different. All great.

Here's what the 4-4-2 Package includes: FE2 suspension with heavy-duty front and rear stabilizer bars; wide 14 x 7" wheels; louvered hood; special 4-4-2 grille; hood and body paint stripes; 4-4-2 identification. And you can order a Hurst Competition Shifter, if you like.

Engine choice? That's a whole new ballgame, too! A spirited 350-cube 2-barrel V-8 is standard. But you can order a 350

4-barrel. Or a 455-cubic-incher with 4-barrels, flared dual exhaust outlets, and a specially sculptured rear bumper. Or order our top package, the W-30 with a dual-intake fiberglass hood and a factory-blueprinted 455 Cold-Air V-8!

The point is this: Now you can "pack up" and go 4-4-2 in more ways than ever. And you can do it for less! Go do so—at your nearest Olds dealer's.

THE PACKAGE DEAL 4-4-2

OLDSMOBILE
ALWAYS A STEP AHEAD

CHAPTER 3

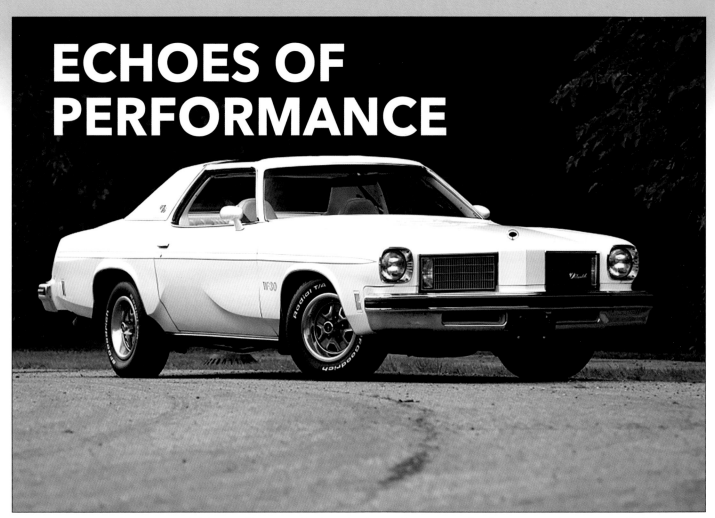

The 1975 Hurst/Olds was available in offsetting Black and White. This Hurst/Olds has the mighty 455 underhood. (Photo Courtesy Judy Badgley)

When General Motors released the 1973 model year A-platform vehicles, a new look debuted. Originally, the new frame and body shell was to have debuted as a 1972 model, but a lengthy autoworkers strike slid that date back a year. All GM divisions except Cadillac used the all-new platform as the basis for their mainstream coupes, sedans, and station wagons.

1973: End Times

Work on the new body started in 1970, when there were plenty of unanswered questions regarding the increasingly strict safety regulations emanating from the government. New bumper standards forced the auto manufacturers to quickly equip new vehicles with what looked like chrome-plated railroad ties. Massive append-ages hung off the front for the 1973 models, and starting in 1974, the rear of the car wore the huge bumper too. Oldsmobile was able to style its bumpers into a slimmer design, but they still looked like add-ons. Due to the new regulations, convertibles were not offered.

Long and Sleek

The weight of the cars ballooned with the new bumpers (300 pounds) and additional mandated rein-forcements within the structure. As engine power was evaporating due to increasingly stringent emissions regulations, performance figures plunged. Oldsmobile used the Colonnade (GM speak for the body design using fixed rear windows and frameless door windows) design that was shaped by Oldsmobile designer Lou Casillo's team as the basis for the Cutlass line, which was still tremendously popular in the showroom.

In 1970, Casillo's group began working on the next-generation Cutlass, paying a lot of attention to the upcoming 5-mph bumpers. This design was used through the 1977 model year. Riding on a 112-inch wheelbase, it was a graceful design with its two doors being 5 feet long and heavy. Sedans and station wagons used a 116-inch frame. Forthcoming federal regulations regarding vehicle roll-over protection led the Oldsmobile design team to equip the new A-platform with a reinforced roof. By eliminating pillarless coupes and fitting a fixed B-pillar and rear side window, the greenhouse structure was strengthened.

W-29 Appearance Package (4-4-2)

Performance enthusiasts weren't completely left out in the cold. The 4-4-2, while now a W-29 appearance and handling package, could be had with two engines: a 350-ci V-8 with a 4-barrel carb and the torque-happy 455 mill, which also had a 4-barrel on top. The compression ratio was now 8.5:1, allowing the cars to use regular unleaded fuel. Underpinnings included heavy-duty FE2 suspension, front and rear anti-roll bars, a fiberglass hood with nonfunctional louvers, and blacked-out grille treatment. There was no W-30 offered for 1973.

Generating the rotational energy for the 4-4-2 was the $137 RPO L75 V-code 455-ci engine. Rated at 270 hp at 4,200 rpm, it churned out 370 ft-lbs of torque at 3,200 rpm when mated with the manual transmission. That's more than enough to leave long black lines on the pavement.

One manual transmission was available: an optional Muncie M20 wide-ratio 4-speed. This was the last year for a 4-speed manual transmission (L75 + M20 carried over from 1972) in the A-Body. For folks preferring an automatic, the trusty M40 Turbo Hydra-matic 400 was the standard transmission, which was the only transmission available in the Hurst/Olds. When the L75 engine was bolted to the automatic and air-conditioning was installed, the Turbo Hydra-matic was coded *OD*, and horsepower was rated at 250. Automatic-equipped, non-air-conditioned Hurst/Olds and cars without air-conditioning used an OW-code box in 1973.

On the drag strip, a 1973 Cutlass with this powerplant clocked in at 14.90 seconds at 97 mph. Top speed was 120 mph. That's a very respectable set of numbers for 1973!

The Hurst/Olds

The Hurst/Olds was alive and kicking, and 1,097 were constructed from 1973 Cutlass S models. Oldsmobile shipped Cutlass Ss to Hurst's Ferndale, Michigan, facility, where modifications were done. Two colors were available: Ebony Black with gold trim or Cameo White with gold

trim, and this was the first year that two color schemes were offered. Hurst went the extra mile painting the two prototype cars, as the stripes were painted on. The production cars used decals. Body modifications were pretty much limited to plastic trim fitted to the inside and outside of the opera windows on the C-pillar to create a smaller window, complete with a tiny H/O decal.

The H/Os were fitted with 455 Rocket V-8 engines containing some W-30 internals, such as valves and springs. All V-code H/Os used KA-heads that were topped with a 750-cfm Rochester Quadrajet carburetor that was topped with a dual-snorkel air cleaner housing on V-code engines only. Functional dual exhaust vented spent gases to the atmosphere. If the car was equipped with air-conditioning, a regular L75 engine was installed and fitted with J-code heads.

A W-based air-induction system from the 1973 W-30 was planned for 1973, but last-minute emissions regulations took that feature off the table. If the Hurst/Olds was equipped with air-conditioning, it was an RPO W-45 U-code engine rated at 250 hp with a trans code of *OD*, and it used a gearset of 3.08:1. Without air-conditioning, the V-code powerplant was also called the RPO W-45. Some Hurst literature mentioned a W-46, but that nomenclature was not used by Oldsmobile.

The air-conditioning-free version was listed as delivering 270 hp, and inside the differential was a set of 3.23:1 gears. Oldsmobile slipped an aggressive camshaft into the W-45 (286/287 degrees of duration and 0.472-inches of lift) with 2.07-inch intake valves and 1.62-inch exhaust valves. Oldsmobile slipped a windage tray into the oil pan of W-45-equipped engines. All of the H/Os in 1973 used Turbo Hydra-matic 400 3-speed automatic transmission controlled by a Hurst Dual Gate floor-mounted shifter. The H/O's OW-code transmission used a 3,000-rpm stall-speed torque converter.

The standard suspension was the capable FE2 setup. With a heavy foot, respectable numbers were still possible; 0-60 mph took 6.5 seconds, and the quarter-mile was covered in 14.90 mph at 97 mph. Top speed was around 120 mph.

The Cutlass line sold well in 1973 with 219,857 rolling down the assembly line. However, the future of Oldsmobile performance in general was not encouraging. Model year 1974 would disappoint hardcore gearheads. But the overall sales of the Cutlass in 1973 told the division's executives that they were onto a growing trend, supplying stylish midsize cars that delivered adequate performance and economy.

The 1974 Hurst/Olds W-30 was a handsome, well-proportioned vehicle. Included with the W-30 package was a dual-snorkel air cleaner, Rallye suspension, heavy-duty cooling, a center console, power disc brakes, high-energy ignition (HEI), and a custom sport steering wheel. SSII wheels were standard with the Hurst/Olds option.

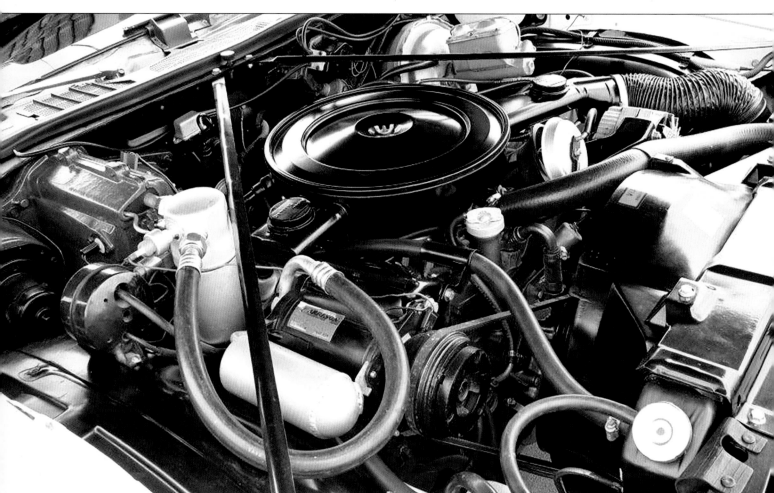

Beneath all of the tubing and the air cleaner was a 455-ci Rocket V-8, setting the 1974 Hurst/Olds W-30 apart from its less-stout contemporaries. Rated at 230 net hp and 370 ft-lbs of torque, it found its way into 380 of the 1,800 H/Os that were built that year.

1974: Going, Going . . .

Somehow, the 4-4-2 was still available. And it could be had with a 455-ci engine. That was the good news. It was still an option package on the Cutlass and Cutlass S. Unfortunately, a manual transmission was no longer available. The 455-ci L76 big-block powerplant that was installed in the Hurst/Olds, ostensibly labeled a W-30, was rated at 275 net hp. But after a one-year hiatus, the W-30 decal was back on the side of a Cutlass fender. The 455-ci L75 option offered in the Cutlass generated 230 hp.

Once more, Oldsmobile paced the Indianapolis 500-Mile Race. It was a Hurst/Olds equipped with a 455-ci engine that Jim Rathmann piloted around the Brickyard. The commemorative versions available in showrooms sold well, with 1,851 units rolling across the curb. Of those, 380 were denoted as Rocket W-30s equipped with the 455. The size of the W-30 callouts on the side of the fenders and in the front grille were impressive; they were readable at 50 paces.

The W-30 package included an impressive list of equipment, including a sport steering wheel, a sport console, 15-inch rims, power front disc brakes, chrome exhaust tips (borrowed from an earlier-model Corvette), a dual-snorkel air cleaner, Rallye suspension, heavy-duty cooling, a 3.42:1 rear axle ratio, and an HEI. Non-W-30s H/Os rode on 14-inch wheels. The remaining vehicles were fitted with the 350-ci engine, which delivered 180 hp with a single exhaust system (K in VIN) or 200 hp when equipped with dual exhaust (M in VIN). This was the only engine available in California. Performance was ebbing away, and the worst was yet to come. However, the Cutlass line was very popular with buyers, as 43 percent of total Oldsmobile sales for 1974 were Cutlasses.

1975: W Still Around–Just

In an era where bigger was worse, the L74 455-ci engine was still available in the Oldsmobile A-Body. It continued to wear the W-30 badging, but with a rating of 190 hp and 350 ft-lbs of torque, it wasn't exactly holding up the banner for high performance. Of course, in 1975, nothing new was. This was the first year for catalytic converters on Oldsmobiles, and a single-pipe exhaust was used—more power siphoned off.

W-25

Another engine wore a W: the W-25. This L34 engine displaced 350 ci and promised to spit out 170 hp and 275 ft-lbs of torque. Both engines could be had in any Cutlass

The 1975 Hurst/Olds Cutlass Supreme was a well-proportioned personal car that came in two flavors: a 455-ci engine labeled W-30 and a 350-ci version coded W-25. Both engines were available in the full Cutlass line, but in Hurst/Olds guise, they wore familiar nomenclature.

PACING THE BIG RACE

In the world of American motorsports, one race has captured the imagination of race fans like no other. The 500-Mile Race at the Indianapolis Motor Speedway is the event that can propel a racer and his or her team into immortality. Over the decades, manufacturers have capitalized on the worldwide exposure to justify supplying pace cars to the race. Over the life of Oldsmobile, 11 races were started with an Oldsmobile product leading the gaggle of straining race cars.

The first race that saw Oldsmobile in front of the pack was the 1949 race with a maroon 1949 Rocket 88 convertible. Three-time race winner (1937, 1939, and 1940) Wilbur Shaw, accompanied by Oldsmobile Chief Engineer Jack Wolfram, handled the car with aplomb.

Indianapolis wasn't the only venue for which Oldsmobile fronted a pace car. In 1957, a new Oldsmobile multiple-carburetor J2-powered 300-hp Golden Rocket 88 Holiday Coupe acted as the honorary pace car at the Pikes Peak Hill Climb on July 4, 1957, driven by Lloyd Faddis.

As the years went by, more Oldsmobiles were pressed into duty at the Brickyard, such as the 1960 Ninety-Eight driven by race winner (1957) Sam Hanks. Oldsmobile was then absent until 1970, when a

Oldsmobile paced the Indianapolis 500 four times in the 1970s, more than any other manufacturer. Linda Vaughn poses with her personal 1972 Hurst Olds. The 1972 race marked the second time Oldsmobile paced the race in the 1970s. (Photo Courtesy Linda Vaughn)

The Colonnade bodystyle debuted in 1973, and for 1974, Oldsmobile and Hurst teamed up again to celebrate the pacing of the Indianapolis 500-Mile Race. Oldsmobile brought back the vaunted W-30 moniker to use with the Big Dog package. Attention-grabbing graphics were standard.

4-4-2 convertible driven by race winner Rodger Ward (1959 and 1962) slipped onto the track. The Porcelain White car had its black and red stripes painted on.

The ragtop was modified by Oldsmobile with essentially a W-30 setup. The pace car used a 3.42:1 ratio rear end and a Turbo Hydra-matic 400 3-speed automatic transmission. The stock rear drum brakes were replaced with units sourced from a Vista Cruiser station wagon. The bigger brakes gave the pace car the ability to shed speed quickly as it entered pit row. Oldsmobile sold replicas (RPO Y74) through its dealers, and they were built in modest quantities: 624 convertibles (all non-W-30s) of which 358 were Cutlass Supremes, and those remaining were 4-4-2s and 355 hardtops.

Only two years later, another Oldsmobile was in the spotlight: a 1972 Cameo White Hurst/Olds piloted by 1960 race winner Jim Rathmann. Because of the debacle in the pits with the 1971 Dodge Challenger pace car crashing into a photographer stand during the 1971 race, no manufacturer wanted to touch the 1972 Indianapolis 500-Mile Race with a pace car. The crew at Hurst approached the Indianapolis Motor Speedway and suggested that a Hurst/Olds would be a viable alternative to a factory entry. The Speedway agreed, and Oldsmobile was once again leading the pack. This was the first time that a non-manufacturer supplied the vehicles needed for the big race.

Hurst/Oldsmobile built 130 convertibles and 499 hardtop replicas. Most of them used the 270-hp 455-ci engine instead of the 300-hp mill in the actual pace car. Just 10 W-30 convertible pace car replicas were constructed. Hurst installed a Hurst-branded aluminum intake manifold and a high-lift camshaft to the cars, as well as a W-25 fiberglass ram air hood. Of the 499 hardtops, 220 were fitted with an optional sunroof.

Then it happened again in 1974 with another Cameo White Hurst/Olds W-30 hurtling around the 2.5-mile track with Jim Rathmann again behind the wheel. Because of the pace car incident in 1971, the Indianapolis Motor Speedway demanded that racers be behind the wheel, and this edict was in force for quite a few years.

PACING THE BIG RACE *CONTINUED*

It wouldn't be a Hurst/Olds without a Hurst shifter. In the 1974 Hurst/Olds W-30, just one transmission was available: the Turbo Hydra-matic 400 3-speed automatic. The standard rear-axle ratio was 3.23:1.

Because there were no convertibles being built by Olds, the top was cut off, leaving a Targa band. Replicas were available at dealers. Hurst/Olds built 1,851 vehicles, which was broken down as 380 W-30s, 1,420 Y77s, 42 Hurst/Olds Delta 88s, 6 Custom Cruisers, 2 actual pace cars, and 1 four-door Cutlass for a total of 1,851 units. The remaining cars used the 350-ci V-8.

Fast-forward to 1977 and Oldsmobile was out front again, this time using a Delta 88 Royale driven by actor James Garner (a.k.a. James Rockford). Replicas of the car were available for sale in dealerships, and RPO W-44, a $914 option, was not for the introvert. A black/silver paint scheme with red accent striping guaranteed that the driver would stand out. Blacked-out exterior trim included the grille, door handle inserts, headlamp surround, door/window frames, and taillight housings. An aluminum hood was used, as well as red sport wheels surrounded by GR-70/15 raised white-letter tires. For buyers seeking yet more attention, RPO W-43 (a $40 option), put a pair of door decals and two sail panel Indy track decals in the trunk, which were to be applied at the owner's discretion. The actual pace car used a Targa top feature that wasn't available on any of the 2,400 replicas.

Oldsmobile's next time crossing the Yard of Bricks was in 1985 with a Candy Red Metallic Calais 500 convertible doing the honors. James Garner once again handled driving duties, this time with a 215-hp 4-cylinder engine pulling the car around the track. Oldsmobile built 2,998 replicas, all coupes.

The marque was on the track again in 1988 with the new Cutlass Supreme. The pace car, driven by pilot Chuck Yeager, was a convertible. Oldsmobile built 250 replicas, of which 200 were coupes and 50 were ragtops. This is significant, as Oldsmobile didn't make a production convertible available until 1990.

A new era dawned at the historic track during the 1997 race, as a Pearl White Oldsmobile Aurora set the pace. This was the first time a front-wheel-drive car led the field, and it was driven by three-time race winner Johnny Rutherford (1974, 1976, and 1980). The Aurora engine was the Big Dog powerplant in the Indy Racing League at the time, and it made marketing sense to have that engine in the pace car. Oldsmobile didn't build any replica of this car.

Another Aurora was tapped for pacing the 2001 event. The red four-door powered by a 4.0L Aurora V-8 had actor Anthony Edwards, known as *Goose* in the movie *Top Gun*, keeping the car on the hard top. Again, Oldsmobile refrained from selling any replicas.

Oldsmobile scored another first during the 2002 Indianapolis 500-Mile Race when it supplied the first SUV to pace the race. A Bravada was prepared by the factory and was able to hold 140 mph using a Vortec 4200 inline 6-cylinder engine cracking out 270 hp. Elaine Irwin, then-wife of singer John Mellencamp, drove the Bravada in front of the race cars. This was Oldsmobile's last turn on that stage, as the division's last vehicle, a dark metallic cherry red Alero, rolled off the assembly line on April 29, 2004, which ended a 106-year run.

Desirable SSII steel wheels were standard on the 1974 Hurst/Olds W-30. The wheel size was 14x7 inches and consisted of three parts: the wheel proper, center cap, and polished trim ring.

Boasting 170 hp and 275 ft-lbs of torque from the RPO L34 350-ci engine's 8.1:1 compression ratio meant that the rear tires were safe from long smoky burnouts. This was the first year of Oldsmobile fitting catalytic converters onto its cars, and for 1975, the exhaust was now a single system.

model. One transmission was used in 1975, the Turbo Hydra-matic 350 3-speed automatic.

The 4-4-2 option was available on both the Cutlass and the Cutlass S. For the first time, a 6-cylinder engine was standard for the 4-4-2. It was the 250-ci inline 6-cylinder unit sourced from Chevrolet. The vast majority of Cutlass buyers stepped away from the opportunity to take a 6-cylinder Cutlass home. Instead, buyers opting for more power could order the base Cutlass (model F37) or a Cutlass S (model G37). Oldsmobile built 6,227 4-4-2s for the 1975 model year, and the breakdown was 212 F37s and 6,015 G37s. Radial tires were now standard on the Cutlass, which helped handling.

W-30

The W-30 option was still available, and for only $128. Checking the box put a T-code L74 455-ci Oldsmobile engine under the long hood. This engine was available in any model Cutlass for 1975. All W-30s in 1975 used J-code heads.

Other features within the W-30 package included Rallye suspension, a sport steering wheel, dual snorkel air cleaner, heavy-duty cooling system, power front disc brakes, a gauge package, high-energy ignition (HEI), and the Turbo Hydra-matic 400 3-speed automatic transmission with a Hurst Dual Gate shifter. Catalytic converters debuted on the entire Cutlass line in 1975, and for cost considerations, the exhaust system was now a single exhaust. While it was still the top dog in the Oldsmobile engine pecking order, it was hobbled under the weight of infant technologies.

Wearing Super Stock III wheels and its original Uniroyal tires, this 1975 W-25 looks like a time capsule. The inside of the wheels was painted gold to match the trim on the bodywork. The Hurst/Olds package cost $1,095 in 1975, which was not an insubstantial sum when the Cutlass Supreme went for $4,047. However, sales in 1975 for the Hurst/Olds set a record at that time with 2,535 units sold, and W-25s comprised 1,342 of that total.

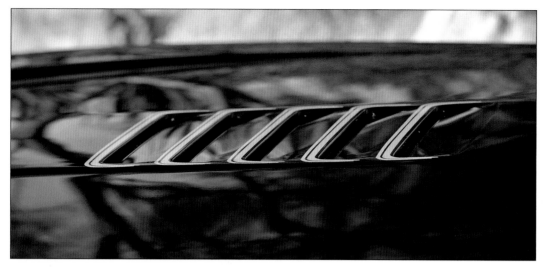

The Hurst/Olds vehicles were never subtle, and the 1975 W-25 was no exception. Faux hood vents edged in gold were a stylistic touch that relieved the large expanse of sheet metal that was the huge hood.

It's inconceivable that a Hurst/Olds would not have a Hurst floor-mounted shifter, and the 1975 W-25 didn't disappoint. In front of the shifter was a Hurst/Olds digital tachometer.

Oldsmobile used the grille from the Cutlass Salon on the 1975 Hurst/Olds W-25 to set it apart visually from the Cutlass Supreme donor car on which the Hurst/Olds was built because all of the gold trim didn't do enough to set the dramatic car apart.

The 1975 Hurst/Olds W-25 was fitted with the 4-4-2's beefy FE2 Rallye Suspension Package, which included heavy-duty shocks, robust anti-sway bars, and high-rate springs. Disc brakes (11 inch) were standard in the front; drum brakes (9.5 inches) were in the rear.

By 1975, comfort was playing a more important part in customer satisfaction, and the Hurst/Olds W-25 used swivel front seats to ease ingress/egress. Except for the seats and the Hurst center console, the interior was basically that of a stock Cutlass Supreme. The front swivel seats used reversible inserts to change the look of the chairs in a flash. The white interior took effort to keep clean.

The Oldsmobile Cutlass line was the best-selling intermediate car in 1975, and for good reason. It was beautifully proportioned, comfortable, quiet, and well-priced. Sales totaled 647,482 units.

The Hurst/Olds

The Hurst/Olds continued into 1975 and was now available only on the formal Cutlass Supreme Salon body. As a way of making up for the lack of traditional performance, every Hurst/Olds was equipped with swivel bucket front seats and removable T-top roof panels. The Hurst T-top feature was introduced in 1975, and the Hurst/Olds and the Buick Free Spirit Pace Car were the first GM cars to use them. Comfort had replaced raw power.

The Hurst/Olds option wasn't cheap; it was $1,095 above the price of the car. In comparison, the 4-4-2 that year cost just $128. Production of the Hurst/Olds was 2,535 units, and 1,193 were W-30 equipped. Production of the W-25 in H/Os was 1,342 units.

The Cutlass line became the biggest-selling component of the entire Oldsmobile line and was the best-selling car in America for 1975. Oldsmobile enjoyed huge sales with the Cutlass in the following years but without a real performance component. Many of the enthusiasts who had lusted after tire-melting performance just a few years prior now had jobs that required a semblance of maturity. Many now had families, and a 365-hp muscle car might not be the best tool to go to the grocery store. The market for brute horsepower had slipped away, and the manufacturers were adjusting their products accordingly.

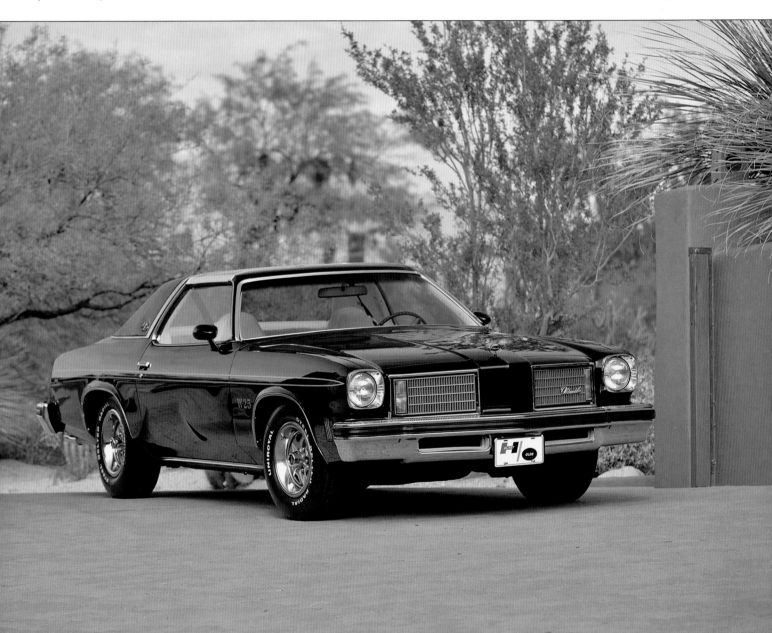

The 1975 Hurst/Olds W-25 used the handsome Colonnade style. This was the first year that General Motors fit Hurst Hatches onto a production car. Detroit was still getting the bugs worked out for gracefully implementing the mandatory 5-mph bumpers.

1976: Missing in Action

This was the final year for the 455-ci engine. It was a shadow of its former self, and not a lot of them were built. The only reference to a W-code was W-29, and this handling package cost $129 and was comprised of thick sway bars, 15x7-inch wide wheels, and heavy-duty springs and shocks. Nothing under the hood was changed with the W-29 package. In fact, any engine offered in the Cutlass S could power a 4-4-2, including the 105-hp 250-ci straight-6. The 4-4-2 option now

"I thought sporty fun cars were gone forever. But the new Olds 442 renewed my faith. Yeah–They built one for me."

It finally happened. Old Faithful broke down.

Not only did I have to walk to the beach for the first time in 5 years, but I was sure I'd never find another car with all that sporty style.

Then I walk by this beautiful, and I mean beautiful, new Cutlass 442. It had a slant-back grille, a big old competition stripe, and all the extras*—super stock wheels, raised white-letter tires, bucket seats, 5-speed transmission. I stuck my head inside to get a better look at the gauges when the guy that owns it comes by. I thought, "uh-oh—here comes a knuckle sandwich." But instead he asks me if I wanted to take it around the block.

It was unreal. That FE2 Rallye suspension gave me that good old cruisin' feelin'. And the guy told me it was even available with a 403—that's the new lighter weight Rocket V-8. On top of everything, it's an Oldsmobile.

Well, I thought they stopped making sporty street machines like that when they stopped making beach movies. But that little ride made me a believer again. I said to myself, "Man—they built one for me."

And who knows—442 might even improve my standing with Sharon.

But that's a whole other story.

*Available options.

Oldsmobile

Can we build one for you?

The thrust of Oldsmobile's performance advertising in 1976 emphasized the Sporty Street Machine and how the vaunted 4-4-2 name set the car apart from its peers. Equipped with a 403-ci engine and side graphics readable at 100 yards, it retained the FE2 suspension, a high-water mark in handling prowess.

was strictly an appearance/handling package. Under the car, the FE2 Rallye suspension worked well to deliver a comfortable ride and competent handling. But the 4-4-2 graphic on each door was huge. This was the era when the perception of performance was all that was left.

With a power output of 190 hp, the 455-ci engine had reached the end of its line. It was available with one transmission: the Turbo 400. It looked like the W series had reached the end of the road. But Oldsmobile knew that the W moniker had legacy horsepower, and it would resurface in a couple of years. The W label was allowed to go dormant rather than destroying a legacy nameplate.

Technology in the mid-1970s wasn't up to the challenge of supplying impressive horsepower with emissions-legal exhaust. Ironically, the Cutlass was still the best-selling American automobile in 1976. Total sales of

495,976 units showed that the country loved the Cutlass line, even if it shied away from performance. In the midst of the disco era, this shouldn't have surprised anyone.

Hurst/Olds built two proposal vehicles in 1976 and another single car in 1977 in an effort to interest General Motors in putting the Hurst/Olds line into production. The corporation declined.

1979: W Is Back (In Lowercase)

Dipping once again into the history trough, Oldsmobile unveiled a Hurst/Olds for 1979 that, at first glance, hit all the right buttons. It wore a handsome two-tone, black/gold paint scheme, and the front fenders wore proud W-30 badging. Using the Cutlass Calais as the donor car, a healthy amount of comfort features were built right in. However, reality stepped in. This was not the same W-30

Equipped for more show than go, the 1979 Hurst/Olds W-30 was a handsome package that actually had some beans beneath the hood. Oldsmobile built just 2,499 W-30s; it was an expensive option, as these cars could cost more than $7,800 when new.

Based on a Cutlass Calais, the 1979 Hurst/Olds W-30 was as good as it got for Oldsmobile for the era. Equipped with an L34 R-code Rocket 350-ci V-8 bolted to an M38 Turbo Hydra-matic 350 3-speed automatic, the powertrain was rated at 170 hp and 275 ft-lbs of torque, which was enough to get the Hurst/Olds W-30 down the drag strip in 16.63 seconds at 83 mph.

that countless gearheads had flogged down a drag strip or between stoplights. No, this version of W-30 consisted of an Oldsmobile-built L34 R-code Rocket 350-ci V-8 rated at 160–170 hp and 275 ft-lbs of torque.

On top of the intake manifold was a 700-cfm Rochester M4MC 4-barrel carburetor. A Turbo Hydra-matic M38 350 automatic was the standard transmission Dual Gate Hurst-Campbell shifter, and the 10-bolt differential was filled with a 2.73:1 gearset, unless the car was sold in California, where the rear axle ratio was a pedestrian 2.56:1. Gold-painted 14x6-inch cast-aluminum sport wheels wrapped in Goodyear PolySteel tires were part of the W-30 package. Just 2,499 H/Os were built for 1979.

Oldsmobile had brought to market a hatchback model (Salon and Salon Brougham) of the Cutlass in 1978. In 1979, it could be outfitted with a 4-4-2 package. Graphics and suspension were the result of checking that box. When installed on the Salon, the 4-4-2 option cost $276; when fitted on the upscale Salon Brougham, the dealer asked for $122. Once again, the Cutlass was America's seller with more than 536,000 sold.

Its performance wasn't catastrophic. It could cover the quarter-mile in 16.63 seconds at 82 mph. General Motors had revised the A-platform for 1978, using a shorter, 108-inch wheelbase. Hurst/Olds production came in at 2,499 units.

American automobile styling in the 1970s went from slippery to boxy in the span of about seven years. The 1979 Hurst/Olds W-30 was firmly in the boxy family, yet it was a well-proportioned design complemented by an attractive two-tone paint scheme. The gold-colored wheels were standard with the W-30 package and are virtually unobtainable today.

The square proportions of the 1979 Hurst/Olds W-30 migrated to the interior but with tasteful results. All the expected creature comforts were in place; after all, this is an Oldsmobile! But the buckets seats, cloaked in grippy fabric, kept you in place during spirited driving. With its stock radial tires and Rallye suspension, the W-30 could find its way around a curve far better than many of its contemporaries. Note the Hurst Dual Gate shifter; no 4-speeds were offered.

Vertical taillights, long a styling cue on Cutlasses, were found on the 1979 Hurst/Olds W-30. The car's formal roofline was a clean design, and the Hurst/Olds paint scheme acted like a good makeup job, minimizing the minuses and accentuating the positives. The subtle gold pinstripe above the rear wheel arch was particularly well done.

1980: Taking a Bow

Little changed from 1979 except that the Hurst/Olds was gone. By removing the Hurst/Olds badging, Oldsmobile created the 4-4-2 W-30 for 1980! Not a lot of them were created—only 886 to be exact, and 346 of those were painted white over gold; 540 were in black and gold. The W-30 option cost $1,255.12, a not-insubstantial sum. This was the only Oldsmobile in 1980 that offered a 350-ci engine. Other Oldsmobile models had to settle for a 307-ci engine or a V-6.

The 4-4-2 option could be added to any Cutlass Calais or Salon. These cars are easily identifiable by the *R* in the VIN. Canada saw 190 units imported with the same L34 350-ci engine and Turbo Hydra-matic automatic transmission and a Dual Gate shifter.

This was the last appearance of the L34 powerplant. Oldsmobile saw the writing on the wall and let the 4-4-2 W-30 nomenclature lie after the 1980 model year. With its passing, an era was over. It came in with a bang and went out with a whimper.

Additional books that may interest you...

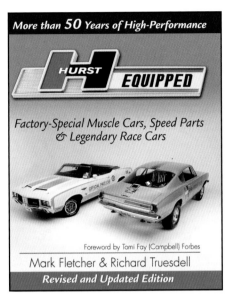
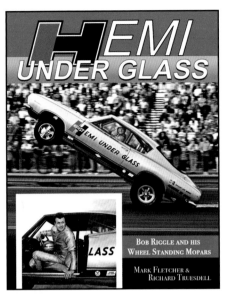

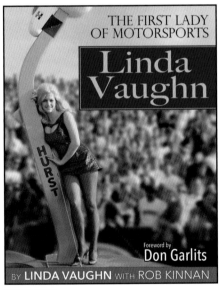